"*The Space Between Us* is an invaluable book. Betty Pries uses her keen intellect, contemplative heart, and years of mediating personal and organizational conflict to guide us into the knowledge and practices that can lead us to peace with ourselves and with the people whose lives intersect our own. She invites us onto a challenging path, which holds the risk of our becoming humbler, wiser, more generous, and more gracious."

 —**REBECCA SLOUGH**, academic dean and professor of worship and the arts emerita at Anabaptist Mennonite Biblical Seminary

"I read this book in the midst of dealing with a significant conflict in our organization, incorporating Betty Pries's methods in how I was working at transformation. Never have I come across a book that weaves together the necessity to engage the deepest sense of oneself with conflict transformation strategy . . . and this book does it through a narrative paradigm. Absolutely brilliant!"

 —**DOUG KLASSEN**, executive minister of Mennonite Church Canada

"*The Space Between Us* offers readers a rich well of practical wisdom about what it means to be human and how to flourish in a world full of pain and conflict. Betty Pries shows us how conflict can be an opportunity for the growth of both individuals and communities. This book is especially important for churches, as it invites us to live more fully into the vibrant, relational life of the Trinity, for which we were created."

 —**C. CHRISTOPHER SMITH**, author of *How the Body of Christ Talks: Recovering the Practice of Conversation in the Church*

"This book is essential reading for anyone navigating conflict. It is a refreshingly holistic and practical approach to both healing oneself and transforming conflict. With exquisite skill and gentle, storied accompaniment, the author explains what could be highly theoretical and philosophical concepts in a most accessible form. This is a handbook for being human, regardless of your spiritual perspective."

—**JENNIFER BALL**, assistant professor of peace and conflict studies at Conrad Grebel University College, University of Waterloo

"In *The Space Between Us*, Betty Pries offers sound conflict management principles and takes the reader much deeper. We are guided toward wisdom so needed in our world today—the ability to manage our defenses *and* differences in order to see and embrace the common humanity of our belovedness. Her work provides a path to greater hope for healing the self and to greater joy for a human community seeking reconciliation."

—**DAVID BOSHART**, president of Anabaptist Mennonite Biblical Seminary

THE

SPACE

BETWEEN

US

Betty Pries

THE

SPACE

BETWEEN

US

CONVERSATIONS *about*
TRANSFORMING CONFLICT

HERALD
P R E S S

Harrisonburg, Virginia

Herald Press
PO Box 866, Harrisonburg, Virginia 22803
www.HeraldPress.com

Library of Congress Cataloging-in-Publication Data
Names: Pries, Betty, author.
Title: The space between us : conversations about transforming conflict /
  Betty Pries.
Description: Harrisonburg, Virginia : Herald Press, 2021. I Includes
  bibliographical references.
Identifiers: LCCN 2021016301 (print) I LCCN 2021016302 (ebook) I ISBN
  9781513808680 (paperback) I ISBN 9781513808697 (hardcover) I ISBN
  9781513808703 (epub)
Subjects: LCSH: Interpersonal conflict--Religious aspects--Christianity. I
  Conflict management--Religious aspects--Christianity. I Interpersonal
  relations--Religious aspects--Christianity. I BISAC: RELIGION /
  Christian Living / Social Issues I RELIGION / Christian Living /
  Spiritual Growth
Classification: LCC BV4597.53.C58 P74 2021 (print) I LCC BV4597.53.C58
  (ebook) I DDC 248.4--dc23
LC record available at https://lccn.loc.gov/2021016301
LC ebook record available at https://lccn.loc.gov/2021016302

Study guides are available for many Herald Press titles at www.HeraldPress.com.

Unless otherwise noted, Scripture text is quoted, with permission, from the *New Revised
Standard Version*, © 1989, Division of Christian Education of the National Council of
Churches of Christ in the United States of America.

25 24 23 22 21   10 9 8 7 6 5 4 3 2 1

For Paul

And for Anya, Thomas, and Stefan

Foreword

I remember a vivid moment of disagreement I experienced at an early age. I had a group of about nine friends in my neighborhood who played together all the time—backyard football, hide-and-seek, and target practice with crab apples. One summer night, participating in our regular shenanigans at our local park, someone suddenly yelled that their Transformer action figure was missing from their duffel bag. The blaming and finger-pointing began. Whatever subtle antagonisms had been under the surface came spewing out like a volcanic eruption. Everyone immediately started taking sides. Factions quickly formed—four kids yelling and another four screaming back. I stood frozen as one kid called me out: "Dan, pick a side or go home." Sadly, we stopped playing together after that day. That rift lasted for three years.

I tell this story because of how obviously childish it is but also because of how common it is for adults. We don't know how to disagree well, whether we're playing in the park or talking about political issues. Conflict often creates two sharply contrasting groups or sets of opinions. It polarizes us—splitting us, creating a chasm. We begin to believe we only have two options: "our side" or "their side." We pick a side and fight until someone wins or gives up. Too often, we Christians switch between passive silence and bitter tirades in the face of our differences. This doesn't seem very Christian to me.

We know this is how wars start, but it's also how churches split, families divide, and longtime friendships dissolve. Can we move beyond this "us versus them" approach to conflict? This polarized approach to conflict is not a new story; it's actually an old one. From the time of the fall, being pitted against each other has plagued God's people—the tales of Cain and Abel, Jacob and Esau, the brothers in the parable of the prodigal son. Such examples are the product of the fall in Genesis 3 and do not come from God's original design for us in Genesis 1. A winner-takes-all political culture reinforces this sin even more so in well-meaning Christians.

The force of conflict has been felt by us all, but few of us have pursued the art and act of transforming conflict. Honestly, it's most often been relegated to professional mediators, whom we see as performing some sort of magic trick. But transforming conflict is not magic; it is a deeply meaningful way to follow Jesus. To grow out of our self-protective survival instincts and mature into rooted ways of addressing the divisions in our life is what we ache for in our human existence. We know this is what it means to more beautifully engage in the world. There may be no other competency that is more essential in our time.

When I apprehended the book you hold in your hands, my soul was given oxygen. With every page, Betty Pries unfolds a wisdom for navigating the space between us. Beyond being a how-to book, this is a manifesto for understanding the "self" and the "other." It is sage guidance for how to be human in a world of divisions. I can't help but imagine how our interpersonal relationships and organizations would change if they nourished themselves with Betty's thoughtful and careful work.

It takes courage to face our fears of conflict. *The Space Between Us* will offer you substantial bravery for that task. We can no longer let the fear settle in and place a wedge in our relationships. So, join me and others who are relearning how to be contemplative with conflict and then experimenting with transformative ways of engagement. It just might change everything around you.

—Dan White Jr.
Author of *Love Over Fear*, coauthor
of *Church as Movement*, and
cofounder of The Kineo Center

Introduction

In a way, this book has been in the making since I first began as a mediator in 1993. While I was learning the trade of how to facilitate tough conversations between people in conflict, I was also paying attention to the micro-moments that allowed meaningful shifts in relationships to occur. And I was noticing the biases and preconceptions people harbored about one another that limited their ability to actually *hear* what the other was saying. I became fascinated by the enduring power of biases and by the moments when a seemingly small gesture functioned like a lever, causing a shift in someone's attitude. During this time, I sensed that transformation between two or more people in conflict was deeply connected to a transformation within the self (and vice versa). Because my work has always involved dealing with conflicts within larger systems (workplaces, communities, and congregations), I also observed that larger systemic patterns within organizations profoundly influence the conflicts that occur between people, and that a shift in the interior condition of individuals within that system—especially leaders—can shape and influence, even transform, systemic organizational patterns. Over the years of my work, I have come to the conclusion that if a transformation of one's interior condition can transform an interpersonal relationship, by extension, this transformation can also transform organizations, perhaps even nations. Likewise, it is also true that a transformation at the systemic level supports both interpersonal change and shifts in the self.

I wanted to understand more about the transformation of the self and, using myself as a test case, began in 1996 meeting with a spiritual director—a nun well into her sixties—who taught me the practice of meditation. Even as a beginner, I sensed that there was something in the discipline of meditation that held great promise for the kind of deep transformation within the self that could allow a relational transformation between two parties, and by extension could change organizational life.

These ideas crystallized for me in late 2004, when I had the privilege of mediating a dispute between two men who had been best friends and colleagues, but whose relationship had deteriorated because of challenges at work, to the degree that the two men had become brutal enemies. The conflict had become so difficult that one man, Alec,¹ saw no way out other than to secure a job transfer to another city, allowing him and his family to start over again in another location. This worked well until, for a variety of reasons, Alec was forced to relocate again, back to his original city, and more crucially, back to the same job and the same colleagues as before. Alec and his former friend/enemy, Roy, were now back in the same workspace. The company, fearing a repeat of the conflict that had existed between the men before, chose to act preemptively by sending Roy and Alec to mediation shortly after the restart of their working relationship.

One could say that my co-mediator and I were mostly observers to what occurred in the mediation room that day.

Alec led the way so graciously and so powerfully that, in a sense, Roy had no choice but to respond in kind. Occasionally, my co-mediator and I asked questions or redirected the conversation; most often, however, our task focused on not getting in the way. In the ten years that Alec had lived away, he received counseling and did significant soul searching. By his own admission, Alec's time away had changed him. I have rarely met anyone who has taken responsibility for their part in a conflict more cleanly and more thoroughly than Alec. Alec did this without demanding the same from Roy—he simply focused on what was his to address. And he offered Roy both grace and forgiveness. Something in Roy was set free when this occurred. He, too, took responsibility for his part and, mirroring Alec, he offered grace and forgiveness to Alec. After this exchange, our mediation focused primarily on how to manage the colleagues around Alec and Roy who had taken pleasure in watching them fight—and who now appeared to want the fight between them to start again.

As I drove home from the mediation between Roy and Alec, my thoughts returned to the nature of transformation. By all accounts, it was a successful mediation. In this case, however, success had little to do with the mediation process or our role as mediators. Instead, success was almost entirely driven by Alec's transformation *prior* to mediation. And while I do not recall whether Alec engaged in a contemplative practice like meditation, his personal transformation mirrored my own experiences with meditation. Transformation within the self has the power to profoundly transform interpersonal relationships.

This book draws on the disciplines of both conflict transformation and contemplative spirituality to explore the connection between the transformation of the self and its influence on the transformation of interpersonal relationships and inter-group relationships. To be clear: This book is *not* suggesting that the transformation of one's self is the only avenue for transforming conflict. Indeed, fixing challenging or inequitable organizational dynamics can also have a positive and profound impact on interpersonal and intergroup conflict. After all, an important saying states, "To solve conflict, turn people problems into situation problems." In my work, I regularly address conflict by helping to strengthen an organization's "situation problems"—clarifying roles and responsibilities; rebuilding a sense of vision and purpose; strengthening structures, policies, procedures; clarifying mandates; and so on—in addition to (or instead of) direct conversation about the conflict itself. But that is another book. While in my professional life I regularly lean on dozens of models and images to teach the skills of conflict transformation, that too is another book. *This* book tries to explore the why of conflict, how it is that we find ourselves in conflict in the first place, and how an understanding of personhood alongside corollary spiritual disciplines to support this understanding helps us in transforming our conflict experiences.

This book is written for those interested in the transformation of conflict, for practitioners of conflict transformation, and for spiritual seekers. While my own tradition is Christian and while I draw from it and other traditions in this writing, my hope is that people of all (and no) traditions will be able to translate this material into their own contexts.

If the reader is interested in an academic discourse on this topic, consider reading my PhD thesis or its companion book, both entitled *Bridging the Self-Other Divide: Conflict Transformation and Contemplative Spirituality in Dialogue*. The thesis is available through the Vrije Universiteit Amsterdam;

the book may soon be available through another publisher. The thesis and book cover similar ground to *The Space Between Us* but in significantly more detail and in a more formal fashion.

The chapters that follow are organized around several key themes: Chapter 1 invites the reader to consider the steps that lead us into conflict. Chapter 2 explores how we might understand our experiences of conflict through a metaphor of personhood. Chapter 3 explores several additional themes related to deepening our understanding of our selfhood. Chapter 4 explores the transformation of conflict. And finally, chapter 5 offers a series of spiritual disciplines for navigating our way through conflict.

Transforming conflict is not easy; yet when we embark on a journey of conflict transformation, we may discover new vistas of joy. The space within us is transformed just as the space between us is healed.

Chapter 1

Disagreements and the Escalation of Conflict

All people experience conflict, or at least all people experience differences that could become conflict. Some conflicts involve just a few people; others erupt between or within groups. Some involve just a few key incidents or issues; others emerge in response to deep and systemic injustices. Some conflicts appear to be primarily internal to one person or group; others are complex and multilayered and involve a diverse group of interconnected stakeholders.

Some conflict is so big, it functions like a bulldozer pushing everything else from its path. When this happens, it can feel as though the conflict *consumes* us. The big conflicts in our lives may drive us in circles, but the bulldozer is unable to clear the landscape of our pain. Instead, pain becomes the new soil beneath our feet. When this occurs, our conflicts become so painful that the simple act of breathing can be a difficult task. The tragedy is, the big conflicts of our lives tend to harm us three times: first, in the original incident (or series of incidents); second, as the memory of the conflict takes hold of us and consumes us, influencing everything from our sense of self-worth to our mental functioning and physical health; and third, as *we* become the creators of new conflict pain with the people in our lives in response to the big conflict we have experienced—even if the people with whom we are now in conflict have nothing to do with the original incident. Sadly, the problem with the pain-based soil beneath our feet is that it tends to beget new shoots of conflict—ones that we may participate in creating because the soil beneath our feet has not been healed. It is said, after all, that *pain that is not transformed is transferred.*

Of course, some conflicts are much smaller. These conflicts might just be irksome or petty. They might be easy to shrug off. Or we may find that a host of small conflicts accumulate within and around us to the degree that we find ourselves dying "a death by a thousand cuts."

How do we understand the nature of conflict? What causes us to fall from healthy disagreement into conflict? How might we learn to manage our differences well?

CONFLICT ESCALATION

Definitions

Differences exist in all interpersonal and intergroup relationships. No two people are alike, no two sets of experiences are alike, and no two minds are alike. I think of the word *differences* as a neutral, overarching term that describes the reality that people will see things differently from one another. Differences are woven into the human condition: No person is complete alone and no person is smart alone. Wisdom happens in conversation. Completion, insofar as such a thing is possible, emerges in community. Quite simply, our differences remind us that we need one another for our survival.

In our relationships, differences are often expressed in three ways: disagreement, conflict, and entrenchment, as seen

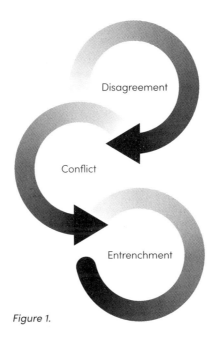

Figure 1.

in figure 1.[1] *Disagreement* is the healthy expression of differences. Disagreements can be intense or muted, difficult or joyful, boisterous or calm. When we disagree, we explore our differences freely with one another—without making those differences personal. We allow ourselves to see the problem as the problem.[2] *Conflict*, in contrast, involves differences that have become personal. We know that we have fallen into conflict when we find ourselves saying things like "He always ..." and "Why does she ... ?" It is not just that we disagree over a problem; it is that we disagree over a problem *and* we believe that the other is the reason we cannot solve the problem. Or we may believe that the other *is* the problem. *Entrenchment* occurs when the conflict-ridden expressions of our differences become cemented in place. Entrenchment is especially painful: we feel victimized by the other, even as the other may feel victimized by us. When we reach the state of entrenchment, the pathway back to a healthy state of disagreement can seem impossible to find.

Disagreement, conflict, and entrenchment can be visualized as existing along a continuum. What begins as disagreement may tip over into conflict, which may tip over into entrenchment. What this means is that when we differ from one another, we know that these differences could take us down the continuum into conflict and, even worse, entrenchment—something most of us like to avoid. As a result, many of us avoid our differences to the degree that we struggle to even know what healthy disagreement looks and feels like. Is it one person giving in? Is it people holding their ground and battling it out? Is it engaging in dialogue with one another? Said most simply: What does it mean to disagree well with one another?

According to organizational health consultant Patrick Lencioni, 80 percent of the workplaces with which he works live in a place of artificial harmony.[3] When we are artificially at peace with one another, we can be afraid to register our differences lest we fall into conflict. We feel compelled to say yes to another person's ideas even against our better judgment. Not only does this result in bad decisions, but it also means we lose the wisdom that a broader perspective gives us. We need one another to make good decisions—and just as importantly, we need to be in dialogue with those with whom we disagree in order to make better-than-good decisions. By definition, we are limited in what we can know, see, and experience. It is in dialogue that we learn new and sometimes important wisdom from opposing perspectives. While it can be tough to talk with those with whom we disagree, and while seeking out disagreement can feel daunting or unnecessary, disagreement itself is essential for any of us to be genuinely wise.

But there is more: When differences emerge in contexts where people feel compelled (because of family culture or organizational norms) to behave like everything is okay, people may publicly behave according to artificial harmony while privately grumbling about the other person, possibly even engaging in mean-spirited personal attacks about the other. In other words, in the other person's presence we behave as though all is well, while in our hearts and minds, or in conversation with our allies, we speak negatively about the other person. Artificial harmony drives conflict because over time, the disparity between what is happening publicly and what we are thinking privately becomes too hard to maintain. The veneer of harmony is simply too thin: our private attacks leak out and become public—often devastatingly so. When people wonder, "How did it get so bad so fast?" I think, "It didn't get so bad so fast." The kindling of disregard was being thrown onto a growing pile of negative feelings for a long time—it is only that a spark finally lit the accumulated kindling.

To counteract the temptation of artificial harmony and the associated fear that disagreement will tip over into conflict, we must learn to differ with one another better. We need better disagreements.

When I was in my mid-twenties, my supervisor was a man in his sixties who loved a good disagreement. Greg and I disagreed happily and actively on a variety of issues. Whenever our conversations became intense, Greg always checked in. "Are we okay?" he would ask. "Did I push too hard?" In my mind, we were always okay because I enjoyed the sparring conversations as much as he did. As we discussed real and tough issues related to our organization, it felt to me as though we were changing the world. When I left the organization several years later, Greg said to me, with a smile on his face, "But with whom will I argue now?"

To this day, I think of my conversations with Greg as one of the best examples of healthy disagreement I have experienced. Our conversations were kind, honest, respectful, and, well, real. We addressed tough issues with one another. We checked in to ensure we had not stepped over any lines. We shared our perspectives freely with one another, and we listened well and carefully to each other's perspective. My conversations with Greg were intense, yet I do not recall any conflicts with him. Our differences never became personal. Why? Because our ability to talk well with one another ensured that neither of us fell into artificial harmony or its corollary behavior, mean-spirited personal attacks, even when we had to have hard conversations with one another.

When people disagree well with one another, they see the problem under consideration as the problem, rather than the other person as the problem. They take time to build and nurture trust with one another. They ensure they understand the problem, they listen to understand one another's perspectives, and they honor one another even as they disagree. People who disagree well check in with each other when the potential for misunderstanding arises to ensure that their differences remain disagreements and do not turn into conflicts. Because good decisions depend on healthy disagreement, people who disagree well actively seek out different perspectives in order to reach more sound conclusions.

Selfhood at risk and the slide into conflict
To more fully understand the shift from disagreement into conflict, it is important to appreciate one of the key drivers

of this shift: our selfhood. As already suggested, the difference between disagreement and conflict is found in whether we see the problem as the problem or the person as the problem. It appears that our inclination to see the other as the problem is driven by our perception that in some way our selfhood is at risk. Our selfhood is most commonly understood as our identity, multilayered and complex, formed by our characteristics and our emotional relationship with our characteristics. Selfhood can also include a deeper inviolable sense of self that is not bound by our characteristics. While we will talk more about selfhood (see chapter 2), the idea here is that we appear to have an inborn inclination to protect our selfhood. To have a self is to be alive. As a result, when we experience our selfhood at risk, fear for our selfhood can awaken powerful emotional reactions within, whether loudly or subtly, consciously or subconsciously. Deep in our being we may perceive that our ideas are not valued, or that our way of being is questioned. We may experience ourselves as being put down, disregarded, or humiliated. We may feel uncertain about the strength of our argument; believe that our authority is threatened by the disagreement; or be reminded of older conflicts in our lives that left us wounded.

Selfhood at risk reveals itself in myriad ways. Practically, when we experience our selfhood at risk, we become defensive. For many, this looks like quickened speech, a racing heart, a turned stomach, and an anxiety-laced tone of voice. Others remain distant, rooting themselves in logic in order to appear cool—and to avoid a turbulent inner emotional reality. In these moments it is as though our mind and body say to us, "I cannot be seen as lesser than"; "I feel at risk"; "Disagreement makes me anxious"; or, "I know I can't win that argument so I must switch it." Or we may feel a need to control the conversation: "If I allow feelings in, I will become uncomfortable." A sharp word, a desire to withdraw, changing the subject—these reactions are less about solving the problem and more about defending or protecting one's selfhood. Frequently, we are simply not well-practiced in the discipline of focusing on the problem as the problem. We have become accustomed to seeing another's personhood as the problem, and so we set off in this direction, unwittingly awakening the other's defensiveness. Inner panic now emerges for the other: this person too experiences selfhood at risk. When this occurs, it as though a lead domino has been tipped and a cascade of tumbling tiles falls, launching us from disagreement into conflict.

Several years ago, a leader of an organization asked me to coach him regarding a challenge he was struggling with. He had noticed that when people disagreed with him, he tended to take their disagreement personally, limiting his ability to have important conversations with his colleagues. He wanted to change this. After he shared his dilemma with me, I asked him, "When you share an idea, where do you hold it? Do you hold it close to your chest, near to your sense of identity, or do you hold it at arm's length?" The leader offered that indeed, he tended to hold his ideas close, aligning his opinions with his sense of identity. Thus, when anyone pushed back on one of his ideas, he experienced that person as pushing back on his personhood. Said otherwise, whenever his colleagues disagreed with him, he experienced his selfhood as being at risk. I picked up a mug that was on the table between us and offered this suggestion: "What if you allow this mug to be the container that holds all your ideas? When you meet with your colleagues, always bring your mug along. Put the mug between you and your colleague—at arm's length, away from your chest and your sense of selfhood. (Your colleague doesn't need to know why the mug is there—virtually everyone carries mugs to meetings!) When you describe your ideas to your colleagues, imagine putting your ideas in the mug. When your colleagues comment on your ideas, put their comments in the mug as well. Allow the mug to be the container that holds your discussions regarding hard topics and differences of opinion—and always keep the mug at arm's length. Your differences of opinion are just that, differences. They are not about your selfhood, or about the selfhood of the other person. When we remember that, we do not need to become defensive."

While each person's situation is unique, that leader is not alone in his struggle. Most of us shift from healthy disagreement into conflict whenever we experience our selfhood as being at risk in some way. And many of us align our identity with our ideas, just as we align others' identity with their ideas, limiting our ability to give and receive feedback well. Not only is our selfhood at risk, but so also is theirs. Putting the mug between us is really just a metaphor, but its intention and purpose is great: to disagree well, we must remember that our personhood (and that of others) is not at risk.

The us-them frame

When we regard our selfhood as at risk, we quickly fall into what is sometimes called the us-them frame.[4] This frame describes the emerging stratification of self and other into categories of "greater than" and "lesser than," good and bad, right and wrong. It is most easily visualized according to table 1.

The us-them way of regarding the world allows us to justify our actions while condemning the actions of the other. Once we have fallen into this prison, there is no way out. No action by the other can ever redeem the other in our eyes: there is

Table 1. The us–them frame

	Action deemed to be good	Action deemed to be bad
Us	▶ If we commit an action deemed as good, it reflects our lovely character. ▶ A good action by a member of our group reflects the character of the group as a whole.	▶ If we commit an action deemed as bad, it is because we were forced into it—we didn't mean it—or because we were having a bad day. Our bad action is situational—it is driven by context. ▶ A bad action by a member of our group is a one-off.
Them	▶ If they commit an action deemed as good, it is because they were forced into it—they didn't mean it—or because they were having an unusual day. Their good action is situational—it is driven by context. ▶ A good action by a member of their group is a one-off.	▶ If they commit an action deemed as bad, it reflects their unsavory character. ▶ A bad action by a member of their group reflects the character of the group as a whole.

always an explanation that places the other in the category of "bad." Conversely, the other can never hold us accountable: our self-justification releases us from any responsibility for the actions we have taken.

The us-them frame organizes our relationships according to a victim-villain worldview. While we may not be genuinely victimized, we nonetheless see ourselves as targeted by the other, or as having less power than the other, because of the other's actions. This feels odd, especially if the person is someone with whom we have had a good relationship. Alternately, we may place others in the category of "them" because their worldview differs from ours. Perhaps they vote differently or perhaps they harbor ideas we find distasteful.

Perhaps they lead our organizations but do not act as we believe they must. Maybe they simply look, sound, and act different from us. The us-them frame can take up residence in our souls in myriad ways.

When we fall into the us-them frame, our brain must fill in data to justify how this has come to pass. We observe patterns in the other that allow us to say to ourselves, "She is always like that" or, "He is so aggressive." While there may be a kernel of truth to our assessment, not only is no one "always like that," but we have now labeled the other according to our assumptions about that person's character rather than describing an action the person has taken.

Our brain now looks for additional data to confirm our growing commitment to the us-them frame. No longer is it simply that we cannot find a solution to our problem in relation to the other person; now the problem is how the person walks, the person's accent, how the person shows up at meetings, and so on. We become annoyed with the other's personhood—quirks of personality and ways of being that have little to do with the problem we are trying to solve.

When we regard the other—whomever the other might be—through the lens provided by the us-them frame, we easily miss that our disregard for the other is not actually about the other's "bad" action but more accurately about the pernicious reality that we have placed the other in the category of "them." We have "otherized" the other. Unfortunately, the step from otherizing to dehumanizing the other is a very short one. When dehumanizing occurs, we are able to justify all manner of behavior toward the other simply because the person is other.

Several years ago, I was talking with a university student after a class I had given about this model. My student belongs to an ethnic group that, in another part of the world, has been in a long, protracted, and deadly conflict with another ethnic group. He stated, "But my people really do want peace. The other people don't." I asked how he knew this. He related that individuals from the other side had recently created a skirmish contributing to unrest in their region of the world. I listened and acknowledged the pain of this recent event. Then I shared that I was also aware of recent skirmishes created by people from his ethnic group, and that I was personally aware of people on both sides of this conflict who desperately wanted and acted for peace. My student countered, "Yes, there are one-offs on their side who want peace, and there are one-offs on our side who do not want peace, but overall my people want peace and their people do not." Gently, I reminded my student that he had just proved the point of the us-them frame. My student is not alone. Once our view of the other is caught in the us-them frame, it is difficult to escape the thinking (and behavioral) prison this creates for us.

In an us-them frame, our selfhood becomes somewhat permanently at risk—at least for as long as we reside within an us-them way of thinking. While we may regard our personhood as "good," the fact that the other is "bad" means that so long as we must be in relationship with the other in some fashion, we live in a state of perpetual concern for our emotional or physical safety.

Moreover, most of us know deep in our bones that none of us is entirely good or pure. Over time, upholding the façade of goodness becomes dehumanizing. When we cannot see or acknowledge the harm we have done, or even the much more mundane but less-than-ideal quirks of our personality, we resist the fullness of our humanity—and our vulnerability. This resistance, ironically, pushes us increasingly into feelings of being lesser than, even when our self-talk and public presentation of ourselves is that of being greater than. Without a shift in our stance, to protect ourselves we fall into shame and blame, further entrenching the us-them frame. Our capacity to return to healthy disagreement—and the mutuality of grace that could exist in the space between us—now becomes increasingly limited.

Triangulation, the tipping point, and entrenchment

It is hard to feel like another person's target. It is also hard to carry within us so many feelings of disregard for another person and that person's characteristics. As a result, most of us at some point will talk to a third person or group about our tension with the other. Known most commonly as triangulation, this stage in our developing conflict is when we talk about rather than with the person with whom we are in conflict. While third-party players can help return us to healthy disagreement, we often choose people to vent to whom we believe will be our allies or, at the very least, will confirm our bias that we are right and the other is wrong.

Triangulation goes by many other names: gossip, venting, seeking a second opinion, and so on. Most of our families, friendship circles, workplaces, communities, and congregations accept triangulation as so normal that we hardly recognize it when it occurs; nor do we realize that when we triangulate, we are already well into conflict. Triangulation is highly correlated with artificial harmony: publicly we behave well with the other, while privately we engage with our allies in mean-spirited personal attacks. As others are drawn in, camps begin to form, language within each group tends to become more polarized, and the issues that started the conflict or accumulated during the conflict become distorted as those in conflict, often unknowingly, exaggerate or overfocus on their experiences of conflict.

Perhaps because it is so normal, most groups can engage in triangulation for quite some time before a tipping point is reached. Like the snowflake that finally breaks a branch laden with snow, it is not unusual for a relatively small event to cause a growing accumulation of conflict to erupt. Now what was hidden has become wide open for all to see. The journey from this tipping point to entrenchment is a relatively quick one. New disputes emerge as evidence to justify entrenchment; assumptions regarding the other and the other's intentions are given the status of objective truth; behavior escalates and becomes hostile. At this point, being right is more important than solving the problem or looking good or reasonable to friends and foes alike. Continuing in the conflict itself is now a matter of principle. Enough self-justification abounds to support actions that humiliate, punish, harm, or dehumanize the other. Once individuals and groups reach a tipping point, to resolve the conflict is to betray both oneself and one's allies. Stepping down from one's story is seen as a loss of self.

Deep within those engaged in entrenched conflict there may remain some self-awareness, albeit mostly buried, of their particular contribution to what went awry. While a fear of vulnerability, shame, and blame is present at the beginnings of the us-them frame, over the course of conflict escalation these characteristics become entrenched in one's way of being, limiting one's capacity to meaningfully address conflict, apologize, maintain curiosity, and refocus on the core issues of concern. One could say that as conflict escalates, one moves further and further away from oneself. For those in this space, it can feel as though one's body and mind do not inhabit the same location as one's heart. Mind and body rage

Table 2. Stages of conflict and affiliated goals and behavior

Level	Focus	Behavior
Level 1: Disagreement	*Goal:* To solve the problem. The problem is the problem.	▶ Differences tend to be substantive or procedural in nature. ▶ Trust is strong. Parties are engaged, seek to hear and understand one another, articulate their own views without fear, collaborate, seek greater good. ▶ Differences are actively sought out, seen as normal, valuable.
Level 2a: Conflict and us/them division	*Goal:* To change the mind or character of the other. The person is the problem. Over time, the character of the other is perceived as defective.	▶ Differences awaken psychological needs. ▶ Trust begins to weaken. The self is experienced as being under threat in some way. ▶ Differences are seen as problematic. ▶ Parties self-justify their view of the other as the problem. Assumptions begin regarding the intention of the other.
Level 2b: Conflict and triangulation	*Goal:* To be affirmed for one's perspective of the other as the problem.	▶ The sense of self in conflict with the other creates a sense of vulnerability. This is resolved by drawing in third parties. ▶ As others are drawn in, camps begin to form and the conflict is entrenched. ▶ Language tends to polarize the issues; people distort the issues, exaggerating their experiences of conflict.

Level	Focus	Behavior
Level 2c: Conflict and tipping point/escalatory behavior	*Goal:* Self-preservation at all costs.	▶ The conflict is moving rapidly to entrenchment. New disputes emerge as evidence to justify entrenchment.
	Fight or flight	▶ Assumptions about the other and the other's intentions are given the status of objective truth.
		▶ Tipping point is reached. Hostile and mutually escalating behavior occurs. The self justifies actions that humiliate, punish, or harm the other. Being right is more important than solving the problem or being seen as reasonable. Conflict is a matter of principle.
		▶ Alliances become solidified; leaders of alliances emerge. Resolution is betrayal of both the self and one's allies.
Level 3: Entrenchment Change in social structure	*Goal:* Destroy the other.	▶ The conflict is entrenched.
		▶ Costs of withdrawal are seen to be greater than costs of defeating others; continuing the fight is the only choice; one cannot stop fighting.
		▶ Parties alter social structure to absolutely exclude the other while still maintaining the conflict. Ironically, new disputes may be limited at this point, as contact between the parties is also limited. Memories of old disputes, however, continue to be rehearsed; they become like codes that govern the behavior of the parties.
		▶ Risk of violence. Relationships may never recover.

at whomever "they" are, while inside one's body, the heart suffers, wounded and afraid.

When parties reach the stage of entrenchment, the cost of withdrawal is seen as greater than the cost of conflict. Continuing the fight is the only choice; one cannot stop fighting. In larger social contexts, parties alter their social structure to absolutely exclude the other while still maintaining the conflict. Ironically, new disputes may be limited at this point as contact between the parties is also limited. Memories of old disputes, however, continue to be rehearsed; they become like codes that govern the parties' behavior. At this stage, the risk of violence is real. Relationships may never recover.

Table 2 summarizes the stages of conflict and their affiliated focus and aims and behaviors.

Sadly, many conflicts do not begin at the stage of healthy disagreement but instead take as their starting point triangulation or even entrenchment. The other is disregarded simply for being the other. Even in those conflicts that begin at a healthier state, most individuals and groups do not reach out for help until the conflict is past the tipping point, limiting the possibility of resolution. Now the transformation of conflict seems like a distant and receding horizon. Peacebuilder John Paul Lederach describes deeply conflicted relationships as those "defined by fear, mutual recrimination, and violence." Conflict transformation steps into this rift, seeking to shift even these relationships "toward those characterized by love, mutual respect, and proactive engagement."[5]

DISAGREEING WELL

The practice of presence

While the journey from disagreement to conflict and entrenchment is painful—and sometimes instructive—differences do not need to lead us in this direction. It is possible to disagree well with one another, just as it is possible to shift from conflict back toward healthy disagreement or even harmony. What must we do to disagree well or to return to healthy disagreement or harmony after a season of conflict? It is so tempting to focus on what the other person can change, what the other person has done wrong, and what the other must do for us to be free from the strain of this conflict. This strategy, however, makes us helpless: we cannot know how soon or how well the other will change. This strategy is also not entirely honest. Often, we too have been complicit in the conflict that has arisen. There is more power within us to be change agents in our conflict narratives than we often realize. This power, however, depends on a key and difficult principle: we must practice the discipline of presence; we must engage in the art of noticing.

The discipline of presence is the willingness to pay attention to what is emerging *in us*. When the other speaks, what emotion arises within us? Where does this emotion sit in our bodies? What name do we give this emotion? What memories are triggered by this experience? What biases for or against the other are lurking in our inner spaces? What are we contributing to this situation? What else is going on for us in this moment?

The author Jonathan Haidt proposes that our rational mind is a lot like a rider sitting atop an elephant.[6] The rider is comparatively small and has only relative control over the elephant's decisions. Similarly, our mind has relatively little control over the elephant on which it sits—our emotions, intuition, biases, instincts, and subconscious. When the elephant and rider disagree, the elephant—by sheer size, weight, and power—always wins. In conflict, it appears that the elephant leads; our emotions, intuition, and subconscious realities lead our mind. The rider, our mind, follows along, justifying the decisions the elephant has already made. Unfortunately—and herein lies the rub—our mind tends to live under the illusion that it is in charge, often suppressing or ignoring the elephant on which it sits.

The practice of presence, as it relates to paying attention to what is emerging in us, seeks to bring the rider and the elephant, our mind and our interior world—and our body—back into balance once more. Specifically, being present is about *being present to ourselves.* It is the art of noticing when our body tenses, our voice quickens, our heart races, and our breath becomes shallower. It involves recognizing emotions as they arise, and it involves noticing the nature of these emotions. Is it anger we are experiencing, or fear? Is it a feeling of betrayal or a sense of disorientation? Are we feeling unworthy, or overwhelmed? Judgmental or worried? The art of noticing also includes observing the "recordings" that run through our mind that are less a function of rational thought and more a reflection of both our biases and our old, emotionally driven narratives. It includes paying attention to how our underlying human needs are making themselves felt in our current interaction. In summary, being present to ourselves includes recognizing how in any given disagreement, rightly or wrongly, our interior condition asks us to consider whether our selfhood is at risk.

It may seem that noticing our interior reality should not be difficult. After all, after the many years we have spent in our body, we should be well acquainted with how our body functions and the emotions that occupy our interior space. Often, however, our rider seems to act as though our elephant does not exist. Our elephant may be trumpeting and pawing at the ground, yet our rider carries on in conversation as though we are a rational being free of influence from the emotions, instincts, and biases that in fact drive us. We barrel ahead, launching ourselves headlong from disagreement into conflict with one another, assuming we are still being led by our rational mind, when in reality, our mind now only justifies the decisions our emotions are already making.

Practicing presence involves the discipline of self-awareness, of recognizing the elephant upon which our mind sits. We cannot attend to that which we do not recognize. By noticing and identifying our emotions, our old narratives, and our biases, we can work with this material without being imprisoned by it. We can acknowledge our emotions as our own. For example, in conversation with another, if we are paying attention to our interior space, we may notice that we are becoming anxious. When this occurs, we are advised to speak tenderly to our emotion, engaging it with curiosity: "I see that I am feeling anxious. Why is anxiety arising within me? To what need is this emotion asking me to pay attention? Do I need to be anxious right now? Does my anxiety belong to this interaction or does it belong to a previous, unrelated incident that occurred during my day? How is the larger context influencing my emotions right now? How do I attend to the anxiety arising within me?" When we acknowledge and engage our emotions, our elephant sees that it has done its job. It has alerted us to the concerns it was carrying. Now it can settle, allowing our mind to attend to our emotion, to learn from what our emotion was trying to communicate, while engaging the rational sense once more. If, on the other hand, we do not acknowledge our emotion—or our bias, instincts, intuition, or subconscious interior reality—our mind will believe it is speaking rationally even as our rational conversation becomes laced with more and more unacknowledged, emotionally laden content. This, it appears, is a key driver causing us to regard our selfhood as being at risk and shifting our dialogue from disagreement into conflict.

While the elephant and rider analogy can help us recognize the shift from disagreement into conflict, the analogy becomes especially poignant when we are dealing with deeply painful conflicts. Recently, I was talking with a friend who carries a significant emotional wound because of a traumatic conflict with a colleague. Despite her best efforts and the passage of time, my friend's wound persists. My friend tries to move on but every few months a new experience triggers her old wound, reminding her of her pain once more. In conversation, my friend and I looked for the word that best reflected the nature of her wound. Eventually, we landed on the emotion she was experiencing: it was fear. Once we were able to name this emotion, my friend began to remember early childhood experiences that also involved this same fear. As my friend and I spoke, she observed how fear imprinted itself on her at an early age to the degree that it is often the first emotion that arises when she finds herself slipping from disagreement into conflict. My friend also acknowledged that when in conflict, she rarely describes her conflicts as being about her fear. More often, she, like the rest of us, describes her conflicts as being about the failures of those around her. While it is true that many around my friend have failed her, it is also true that her unnamed and unacknowledged fear has kept her from responding freely in the disagreements in her life.

Our deep wounds can heal. Nonetheless, the emotion associated with our deepest wounds tends to reappear, unbidden, over the course of our lives. The practice of presence involves noticing our emotions as they arise, calling them by their name, and speaking to them; it involves developing a neutral relationship with our emotions. For my friend, it has become about speaking kindly and neutrally to her fear when it arises, "Hello, fear. There you are again. I see you." When she speaks to her fear in this fashion, my friend is no longer hooked by her fear. Fear subsides and she can confidently (and sometimes even joyfully) attend to the conversation in front of her once more.

When we develop a non-anxious and non-dismissive relationship with our emotions, our emotions become like a data bank for us, providing us with important information without enslaving us. Now we can lean into the second expression of the practice of presence: the capacity to be attentive to the other and to the larger context in which our differences occur. When this happens, our capacity to be wise and discerning about the differences before us increases.

Focusing on the problem as the problem

Several years ago, a man named Ben came to me for coaching about a conflict he was having with Morley, his neighbor. Morley wanted to have a fence built between his property and Ben's—an expense he wanted Ben to cover. Ben did not see a need for a fence, but to keep the peace he agreed that a fence was a good idea. Since it was Morley who wanted the fence, Ben believed the cost should be shared fifty-fifty. The conversation between Ben and Morley regarding the fence did not go well. Ben's elephant was triggered, making it hard for him to be present to himself and to Morley. In fact, the conversation escalated to the degree that Ben retreated from the conversation feeling profoundly wounded and afraid. In desperation, Ben called for help. He wanted to better understand what had happened between him and Morley. He also knew he could not avoid Morley for very long. He needed strategies for conversation—and quickly.

When Ben and I met, we reviewed his conversation with Morley, how it had escalated, how Ben's elephant had been triggered, and how the conversation had ended. At some point in the conversation, I asked Ben what the problem was over which the two men were disagreeing. This seems like a question with an obvious answer. In fact, the answer is not as easy to identify as one might assume. From a distance, we can agree that the problem is how to cover the cost of the fence. A secondary problem can be described as the challenge of how Morley and Ben structure a good conversation with one another. In the absence of being present to ourselves, however, these problems are hard to see. In the real-life conundrums of conflict, the temptation to see the other *person* as the problem (rather than the problem as the problem) is great. It so quickly appears as though the conflict *is* the other. It is true of course that personality conflicts and historical tensions between Ben and Morley complexified the problem. The inability of either Ben or Morley to be present to himself also complexified the problem. When Ben expressed his frustration with the situation, he described Morley's many personality deficits: Morley was too quick to anger, too lazy, too unwilling to find work, and too much of a meddler. For his part, Morley accused Ben of being too rigid, too self-centered, too selfish, and too focused on his work. With time and over the course of several conversations, Ben was able to welcome his emotions related to his conflict with Morley. As he attended to his emotions and as his elephant settled, his mind gained perspective once more, allowing him to focus on the core problems he and Morley needed to solve.

When our elephant settles and our rider can function again, we, like Ben, more clearly see the problem over which we are disagreeing. While each disagreement is unique, our "problems as problems" tend to fall into one or more of several categories:

a. a concrete *decision* that must be made (e.g., how Ben and Morley will pay for the fence);

b. expectations regarding how *communication* should happen or should have happened (e.g., harsh words between the two men);

c. an *incident* that needs discussion (e.g., whether Morley's dogs harmed Ben's cat);

d. differences in *information* (e.g., whether Morley and Ben have different data about how much a fence costs and what is permissible according to their city bylaws);

e. expectations regarding the *process* by which decisions are made (e.g., how Ben and Morley will make the fence decision); and

f. differences in *values* (e.g., Ben may prefer open lawn environments; Morley may prefer closed, fenced spaces).

Identifying our problems neutrally and as our key point of focus is critical. By depersonalizing our conflicts while attending to our interior space *at the very same time*, we have better disagreements. We do not fall into the trap of otherizing the other. We—and the other—avoid becoming defensive, our elephant remains calm yet engaged, and our mind remains capable of thinking together with the person with whom we disagree.

The practice of presence alongside focusing on the problem as the problem can be visualized as a step-by-step process. To develop this process, we need to dig into Ben and Morley's story just a little further. Let us assume for a moment that Ben's presence has always annoyed Morley because somehow Ben's professional success awakens old feelings of inadequacy in Morley. Let us also assume that while these feelings are present for Morley, he has worked doggedly to deny them. He believes he simply dislikes Ben and can come up with a thousand reasons why—though no reason really explains the depth of his feelings. From Ben's perspective, it is not so much that Ben dislikes

Morley as it is that he is confused by him. Morley talks in circles and Ben cannot follow his logic. If he is honest with himself, Ben feels somewhat superior to Morley. Ben is accomplished, his life is organized, and he keeps his yard clean—all things that Morley is not or does not do. Ben is annoyed with Morley but lives at arm's length from Morley's world. This, it appears, angers Morley, because in truth Morley would value nothing more than a close friendship with Ben.

With so much backstory, it is easy to see why a simple fence dispute between Ben and Morley is not so simple. The problem the two men share is the fence. For Morley the problem may also be his feelings of inadequacy, and for Ben it is also his feelings of superiority. Notice here that each person's non-fence problems are not so much about the other person as about his own internal emotional processes—yet, in practice, these are expressed as the other person being the problem rather than as a recognition of the problem as located in one's own emotional state. Whether the issue is one of inadequacy or superiority, the fence dispute has placed the selfhood of both men at risk. If either man could recognize his feelings, own them, and release them, he would not experience his selfhood as being at risk, allowing him to return to the fence problem more neutrally, and allowing the two to solve this dispute in a more straightforward manner. This, however, requires a commitment to self-awareness followed by self-regulation—ideally not only after the disagreement has turned to conflict but also amid the disagreement. Unfortunately, this is not the strategy Ben or Morley—or the rest of us—always follows.

Now, using Ben and Morley's story as a springboard, let us complexify the problem even further. Let us assume that Morley becomes so angry with Ben that, in a fit of rage, he yells at Ben, making Ben feel harassed by Morley. What is the real problem now? The problem with how to pay for the fence and how to have a good conversation with one another has not changed. Nor have the backstory dynamics that each man brings to this issue. Now we have an additional problem: How do we deal with the harm created by the intensity of this most recent exchange?

In the scenario above, while the persons involved bear responsibility for their actions and for their underlying feelings that contribute to their actions—and while each contributes to the problem—the other person is never the core problem. The issue remains the problem of the fence payment, complexified by the actions each has taken, and by each man's underlying emotional processes that drive his actions. Morley and Ben could follow a three-step path that would lead them to a healthier disagreement with one another. If Ben and Morley (a) recognize, accept, heal, or transform their own underlying emotional processes; and (b) take responsibility for the actions each has done to create harm; then (c) they can refocus on the fence as the problem—including developing a clear understanding of why each takes the position that he does on the issue of cost. When this happens, Ben and Morley might successfully solve their disagreement over the payment for the fence.

Many people want to jump directly to refocusing on the fence as the problem without doing the hard work of steps A and B. While this can sometimes work as a stopgap measure, more often than not our underlying emotional processes and denial of the harm we have done seep into our attempts to focus on the fence, causing our conversations about the fence to only make matters worse not better. We might blame the other for making the conversation go poorly when, in fact, it is just as likely that our own unresolved emotional processes stand in the way of effective and healthy disagreement. Attending to our underlying emotional processes is a gift we give to ourselves and to others. The more we are aware of, accept, and heal our interior emotional landscape, the more effectively we can engage in healthy disagreements with one another.

Some people might ask, "What if Ben can take this three-step journey but Morley can't? Does this not mean that Ben is held hostage by Morley's unfinished emotional processing?" In my experience, only one person needs to take this three-step journey. While it is always more delightful—and easier—if both parties address their underlying emotional processes, if only one party does so, that party can establish a measure of emotional distance from the overall situation in order to refocus on the problem itself. If Ben is the only one to address his underlying emotional processes, his inner calm can serve as a bridge for Morley, helping Morley focus on the problem as well. Ben now focuses on the problem as problem with the awareness of the emotional constraints placed on the conversation by Morley's unfinished internal conversation. This may make solving the problem more difficult, but it removes the emotional intensity of the situation for Ben, making him more effective in the problem-as-problem conversation.

The three-step path to healthier disagreements is simple, yet profound. If Morley were to follow these three steps, his process might sound like this:

a. I am feeling inadequate around Ben. This is about me, not him. I accept my feelings of inadequacy, and release these feelings.

b. I have spoken harshly to Ben. I take responsibility for these things, regardless of what Ben has done to me. I will apologize to Ben.

c.   I commit to thinking and talking about the fence
     payment. Why is it important to me that Ben pays the
     full fence fee? Because I need the fence for my dogs
     but cannot actually afford to pay the cost of a fence.

a.   (Return to step a.): Not being able to pay for the
     fence makes me feel vulnerable, but my feelings of
     vulnerability are my reality, not Ben's. I will not be
     angry with Ben for my feelings of vulnerability.

The three (plus one) steps that Morley follows to return
to the problem as the problem involve a certain amount of
"homework" or attention to his interior condition (steps a.
and b.). In the world of contemplative spirituality or mindfulness, we talk about this attention as the practice of presence—
being in the now—and paying attention to what is emerging
within. It also involves the practice of taking responsibility
for that which is ours. While we will talk more about how we
attend to our interior condition later—indeed, most of this
book is about these first two steps—for now it is important
to reiterate the significance of the discipline of self-awareness
regarding the drivers of conflict that lurk in our inner spaces.

Turning people problems into situation problems

Beyond attending to our interior condition, there is wisdom
in remembering that our disagreements are deeply influenced
by the context from which they emerge. To disagree well with
one another—and to focus on the problem as the problem
rather than the person as the problem—we are advised to *turn
people problems into situation problems*, considering how the
larger situation has contributed to the problem. It is tempting
to divorce the larger situation from our interior condition, yet
we know that the larger context and our interior condition are

often like mirrors of one another. Situation problems can take up residence in our being, influencing how we act and react to one another. If we can transform a situation problem, our interior condition—our feelings and perspectives about the other—can also be transformed.

Consider, for example, an incident of racism. While an individual may be behind an act of harm, it is also true that a larger social context that accepts, aids, or abets racism undergirds the individual incident of racism. While it is important to address the individual incident of harm, by placing this act in its social context—what we refer to as systemic racism—we can also address the issue at a larger level. Although working at the systemic level may not change each person, we know that transformation at the systemic level also changes behavior at the individual level. It also bears noting that by remembering the larger social context, we also more easily remember the personhood of all of those involved and affected by the individual act of racism: by placing an incident of harm in its larger social context, we gain some understanding of the impact that an accumulation of singular incidents has on the personhood of those on the receiving end of harm. Conversely, when we regard the larger situation behind an act of harm, we more easily find a measure of grace for those who commit acts of harm, allowing us to recall also the personhood of these individuals.

In organizations, community groups, and congregations, the larger situation can include the organizational structure, policies and procedures, the values of the system, its leadership style, and the confluence of issues with which an organization is wrestling. In interpersonal settings, situation problems can include the extenuating circumstances with which those in conflict are wrestling. For example, a person who experienced trauma as a child can be influenced by this experience well into adulthood. A person under unusual levels of stress at work may bring this reality into conflicts at home or on the road.

Situation problems can also include the challenges associated with change. Over the past ten years, I have worked with numerous interpersonal and organizational challenges in a context of change. Change theory suggests that, as people, we will always struggle with change, at least to some degree. Whether we desire the change we are facing or find it uncomfortable, whether it is a change we have chosen or one that is thrust on us, when change happens the rules of life are altered, at least as they relate to the change context. In a sense, change thrusts us back to kindergarten—a time of life when we found everything strange, foreign, and new. And just as on our first day of school, most of us feel at least slightly anxious when encountering change—we don't know what this change will demand of us.

Recently, a colleague was working with an organization deep in conflict. People were angry with one another; sides had been established, and accusations were hurled back and forth. As my colleague looked at the data emerging from the organization, the complaints the sides made about one another simply did not add up to the level of anxiety in the system. Then she tallied the significant changes in the organization over the past five years: a new leader after the retirement of a beloved thirty-year leader; significant organizational growth over the past several years; new rules and regulations based on changes to government policy; a new location; and a substantial number of staff retirements. In addition, this organization was affected by the changes in the larger society—changing social norms, political upheaval, changes in communication patterns related to social media, environmental devastation in the broader community, and most recently, a pandemic. It is no wonder the people were struggling. While the specific conflicts between the parties were real and needed attention, the context of change created a situation problem that significantly affected the parties—adding new dynamics and anxiety to their situation.

Recognizing situation problems for what they are—especially related to change—normalizes the challenges that people experience. It puts specific challenges into a larger context and helps explain why everything appears so overwhelming. This generates profound relief. Knowing why we are overwhelmed allows the world to make sense again. It can also open the door to increased grace for one another: "It isn't that we are bad people, it is because the situation we are in is tricky."

Staying on the same topic

If focusing on the problem as the problem and turning our people problems into situation problems are two strategies for remaining at healthy disagreement, then a third strategy is to actually stay on the same topic as the person or group with whom we are disagreeing. This strategy, like the others, depends on observing what emerges in our interior spaces. Unfortunately, when we become flustered or feel at risk in our disagreements, we tend to obfuscate the issue, changing the conversation into one that we believe we can win. Sometimes it is obvious we are doing this; other times it is so subtle we hardly notice the shift we ourselves are making. For example, Ben might say to Morley: "I am concerned about the way you speak with me," to which Morley might reply, "Yeah, well, I'm concerned about how you always let your cat run into my yard." In this case, Morley has just switched the topic from one issue to another, believing (subconsciously perhaps) that the new topic is one he can win. Morley is obfuscating the issue, changing it just enough that the conversation shifts in his favor.

Consider for a moment another example. When the Black Lives Matter movement emerged, some people responded with the phrase "All lives matter." The latter phrase obfuscates the issue and shifts the argument to one that those opposed to the Black Lives Matter movement can win. It also represents a resistance to looking at the hard issues that have caused the Black Lives Matter movement to emerge. Of course all lives matter—in fact, Black people have never said that all lives do not matter. The issue is that in much of the Western world, two people with identical backgrounds, educations, and life experiences but with two different skin colors will have different social outcomes solely because of the color of their skin—a social outcome that tends to favor light-skinned people over dark-skinned people.[8] As several people stated during the summer of 2020: saying "All lives matter" in response to Black Lives Matter is like watching a house burn and refusing to help put out the fire because all houses, including those not currently burning, matter.

Returning to the Ben and Morley example, it may be true that both Ben and Morley have important concerns—Ben about the way Morley speaks with him, and Morley about Ben's cat. If Ben and Morley talk about their own concern to one another at the same time, both will feel unheard, and likely both will leave the conversation feeling escalated and frustrated. Instead, to disagree well, Ben and Morley are advised to speak first about one topic (such as how Ben speaks to Morley) before shifting to a second topic (such as Morley's concerns with Ben's cat). Staying on the same topic with another person rather than obfuscating the issue takes patience and, at least in some situations, considerable emotional fortitude. The impact is significant: not only are we able to disagree better with one another, but in doing so we also honor one another in the process.

THE BUILDING BLOCKS OF COMMUNICATION AND CONFLICT
Foundational needs
Conflict theory suggests that five foundational needs[9] lie at the core of each person (and each group of persons). These needs are so core to our being that they are woven into the fabric of our individual and collective personhood. Our needs reside in our interior spaces, exerting themselves both in times of joy and in times of conflict. Our needs are not frivolous. They drive our desire for connection; they push us to explore the world; and they help us pursue our sense of purpose. While the expression of foundational needs may vary from one culture to the next, a version of these needs remains present in each person and each group. Our foundational needs can be described as needs for belonging, recognition, self-determination or autonomy, security, and meaning. These needs are so foundational that they are reflected in the words of children: "They're not letting me play" is a need for belonging. "His piece is bigger than mine" is a need for recognition. "I can do it myself" is a need for self-determination. "Mommy, will you hold me" is a need for security. And "But why?" is a need for meaning. Naturally, there are adult versions of each of these needs. Unfortunately, when our foundational needs are not met, we experience a risk to our sense of selfhood (whether individually or collectively). When this occurs and is not caught or addressed, a fall into conflict follows.

Years ago, I was presenting on foundational needs to a congregation when a rather gruff man in the back corner of the room stood up, pointed awkwardly to an image of these needs that I had drawn on the whiteboard, and half shouted: "That's why I've been writing those nasty letters." All the heads in the room turned to look at this man; everyone had a confused look on their faces. The man continued, "I've been looking for belonging." Sending nasty letters does not naturally lead to belonging. And it did not for this man, either. In fact, this man's letters led to exclusion more than belonging. Years later, I learned that this man had had a troubled childhood and had searched for belonging his entire life. Now, toward the end of his life, he had tried once more to achieve belonging, but in all the wrong ways.

The problem with our foundational human needs is that they are so closely tied to our sense of selfhood that we experience our needs as vulnerabilities. It is difficult to articulate a need for belonging. It may be easier to name our need for recognition, but it can be challenging to explain why this need is so important to us. As a result, when people do try to put their needs into words, it comes out awkwardly—or worse, it comes out as conflict. Said otherwise, our bad behavior is sometimes a misguided attempt to express a foundational need. The man in the workshop was looking for belonging but had no idea how to say this to people. He was gruff and aggressive. And beneath that exterior was a wounded man trying to belong to the people in his community.

When I work with conflicted workplaces, well over three-quarters of staff will say they do not receive enough recognition from management. When teenagers and their parents fight, they are often in battle over competing needs for self-determination (on the part of the children) and security (on the part of the parents). When people in movements such as Black Lives Matter protest, they argue that systemic racism upheld by police forces puts the security, recognition, belonging, and self-determination of Black, Indigenous, and people of color at risk.

One of the challenges associated with our foundational needs is that they are often connected to one another while also being in competition with one another. We can form an attachment to a foundational need for ourselves to the degree that we perceive meeting the need of another person as a threat to meeting our own need. Two groups may have a mutual need for security, but one group's avenue for addressing this need may be to maximize its own security while minimizing the other's. One group's need for self-determination may conflict with another group's need for recognition. One person's need for self-determination may cause that person to deny another's need for belonging.

Our needs are wonderfully woven into the fabric of our humanity and are closely associated with our sense of individual and collective selfhood. In healthy disagreement, when selfhood is not at risk, our needs play in the background like the music of our lives. A good conversation can generate satisfying feelings of both belonging and recognition. The resolution of differences can support our need for self-determination and security. Understanding another person or a situation better helps us make sense of the world, satisfying our need for meaning. It is not surprising, then, that when our needs are unmet in some way, we experience our selfhood as being at risk and fall from disagreement into conflict.

It also appears necessary to practice the discipline of noticing for our foundational needs. As we notice the needs emerging within us and accept our needs, we can discern how to attend to our needs at any given moment. It is possible, after all, that our conflict with another person is more about our own unmet needs than about what the other person has or has not done. Alternately, our unmet needs could reflect an important point of concern with respect to our relationship with the other. When we do not recognize our foundational needs, we become like the man who wrote nasty letters—we express our needs in all the wrong ways (including sometimes passive-aggressively), causing us to unnecessarily create or escalate conflict. When we identify our needs and either attend to our need or speak with self-awareness about our needs, we are simply more free. A lightness of being becomes possible for us, allowing us to have better conversations and better disagreements with one another.

Substantive reasoning, process expectations, and foundational needs

Several years ago, I was working with an organization that needed to move to a new location. The administrative leadership and clinical services team had agreed that they would decide their move date together, which they indeed did. Some months before the anticipated move date, the administrative leadership learned new information that caused them to shift the move date forward by several months. Then they called a meeting with the clinical services team to share the news. The conversation did not go well.

During the meeting, the administrative leadership explained that they changed the move date because of new financial information that had emerged. The clinical services team protested, arguing that the administrative leadership had promised a joint decision about the move date. The administrative leaders were incredulous, and threw their hands up in frustration. They were baffled that the clinical team did not see the logic of the changed move date. For their part, the clinical team was equally baffled. To them, the unilateral decision taken by the administrative leaders broke trust: How could the administrative leaders not see this?

The two parties were well into their argument with one another when I arrived for a meeting with them. I listened for a while. Finally, all ten heads turned in my direction, looking for help. I proposed that the two parties were missing each other (like proverbial ships in the night) because they were not, in fact, talking about the same thing. The administrative leaders were offering a substantive logic-driven reason behind a changed move date. The clinical team was raising concerns about due process. And over the course of their argument, foundational needs for both parties were being awakened, in this case, needs for recognition, self-determination, belonging, and security. I am sure that had they been on the outside looking in, as I was, many of those present would have seen that they and their colleagues were arguing about different issues. Unfortunately, when we are inside a conflict, our capacity to think and see clearly can be compromised to the degree that only in hindsight do we recognize what was actually going on.

Substantive reasoning, process expectations, and foundational needs are important building blocks that work together to support good conversation, as reflected in figure 2. Each block is important and plays a critical role in the construction of the conversation: Substantive reasoning represents the rational, logic-based interests behind the position we might take on an issue. Process expectations reflect our interest in due process—our expectations of how a conversation should have gone or should be going. Foundational needs are woven into our human condition and represent the essentials that are critical for our well-being. When we disagree with one another and are stuck, it is worth reviewing whether we are talking

Figure 2.

about the same thing. As with this group, one party could be speaking about the substantive reasons behind its position on a topic, while the other party could be talking about its expectations regarding process—how a conversation has gone or should be going, or how a decision was or should be made.

When we disagree with one another, it is common to think differently from one another at the level of substantive reasoning. This kind of disagreement can be quite enlightening, interesting, and even joyful. In fact, as long as the process is fair, it is common for people to agree to disagree on substantive differences. When at least one of the parties experiences the conversation, the decision-making process, the system, or the relationship as unbalanced or unfair (all of these being process expectations), foundational needs are awakened, driving the disagreement headlong into conflict.

Curiosity

One of the most helpful pieces of advice I first learned about managing the building blocks of communication is to turn judgment into curiosity. A curious stance invites us to ask questions, to be open to the blocks that undergird another's perspective, to believe that there is more to the other person's point of view than we have assumed or can imagine. The more curious we are, the more humble we become. We simply do not know the whole story.

My three favorite "back pocket" words for situations of disagreement or conflict are "Tell me more . . ." When we ask for more information, we do four things at once: we invite accountability, we learn new information, we buy time, and crucially, we meet the other person's need for recognition. A curious "Tell me more" stance invites accountability because conflict has a way of hiding behind generalizations and sweeping statements—including statements about our rationale for the position we have taken on a matter of disagreement. Sweeping statements also tend to cause the other person to cower. More often, generalizations shut down rather than open up conversation. When we ask the other party for more information, the other is invited to back up statements made and to move from generalizations to specifics. Not only does this invite accountability for the statements the other has made, but "Tell me more" gives us more information, allowing us to respond more effectively to the other person. It also buys us time. As we listen, we have time to think, ensuring that our response is, in fact, a response and not a reaction to the other person. Most importantly perhaps, a curious stance satisfies the other's foundational need for recognition. People feel heard when they are invited to say more about the statements they have made. Not only does this de-escalate conflict, but when people feel heard and seen, a connection between self and other is established, increasing the possibility that healthy disagreement and harmony emerge out of our differences.

Curiosity involves not missing the forest for the trees. While speaking from facts rather than conjecture is profoundly helpful, we limit healthy dialogue when we are wedded so strongly to logic or when we become so focused on the accuracy of each word that we miss the meaning behind what the other person is saying. Cross-examination belongs in the courtroom, not the community. To remain at healthy disagreement, we must become deeply curious people, listening for what the other is trying to say, both with words and with the spirit behind the other's words, with regard to the other's substantive concerns and procedural expectations and foundational human needs.

(MIS)COMMUNICATION

Intent, action, and effect

Several years ago, a man named Lou came to me for coaching because of a tricky problem at work. Lou is a custodian for a midsize organization. Ana is a senior manager. On a particularly gloomy and cold January morning, Ana came in to work and noticed that the walkways were not shoveled. She approached Lou in the foyer where several people were standing around, and she loudly asked Lou to clear the walkways. After this exchange, Lou left the building. He called his supervisor from his doctor's office, indicating that he would be on sick leave for several weeks. During my initial conversation with Lou, the following emerged: Lou had been late to work on the day his sick leave began because of an ill child at home. He was about to clear the walkways when Ana walked into the building. According to Lou, Ana was shouting at and maligning Lou as she chastised him for not attending to the walkways. Lou was deeply embarrassed by this exchange. Because Lou experienced Ana's comments so negatively, he assumed that Ana intended to embarrass him in front of their colleagues. By the time Lou came to see me, he had also been told that, according to Ana, because she was cold and shivering when she came into the building, her manner of speech was unnaturally loud on that morning. Because her intentions were positive, Ana assumed that Lou would receive her comments positively. In contrast, because he experienced Ana's comments negatively, Lou assumed she intended to harm him.

Assuming intent based on effect and effect based on intent is the beginning of many misunderstandings. In principle, the conflict between Lou and Ana should be easy to solve. Ana and Lou could simply recognize each other's experiences, apologize to one another for their part in the situation, and resolve the matter. In reality, the conflict between Ana and Lou is much more complex. According to Lou (and corroborated by the human resources director and those present that morning), Ana has a history of making loud and edgy comments to Lou about his work when others are present. Ana also makes less-than-savory comments about Lou when Lou is within earshot. On one occasion when Lou confronted Ana about a comment she made regarding his speech impediment, Ana told Lou he was too sensitive and that she was only trying to be funny. Although Lou has not challenged Ana again, his teeth are on edge whenever he sees Ana. Lou has been deeply wounded by Ana. He does not trust her and, whenever possible, avoids being in Ana's presence.

In times of conflict, our brains tend to review the twists and turns of what happened. As we tell and retell ourselves the story of what occurred, we easily fall into the twin traps of assumption-making and confirmation bias. To better understand this

Figure 3. Intent–action–effect communication

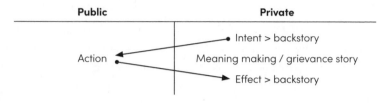

dynamic, consider the intent-action-effect communication model, as seen in figure 3.[10] The elements of this model are as follows:

- Intent: The reason behind an action that is private to the actor.
- Action: A comment, act, or event that is public insofar as it can be heard or seen by both parties.
- Effect: The impact of the action that is private to the receiver.
- Backstory behind intent: The reason behind one's intention. The backstory often has relatively little to do with the immediate situation.
- Backstory behind effect: The reason behind the effect on the receiver. The backstory behind the impact often has little to do with the immediate situation.
- Meaning making or grievance story: The stories we tell ourselves about what happened, about the other person, and the characterizations about one another that grow from these stories.

To make sense of what occurred, we tend to make assumptions about the other person's intent or the effect of our actions on the other person. In a sense this is natural. Because intent and effect reside in the landscape of what is private to the actor and the receiver, if we do not bring intent and effect into the public—that is, if we do not talk about why someone undertook an action or how something affected the other—we are left to make assumptions. Usually when this occurs, we assume the other person's intent based on the effect the person's action had on us, just as we assume the effect of our action based on our intention. In other words, if something affected us negatively, we tend to assume that the other intended for us to be affected negatively; likewise, if we believe that our intent was positive, we tend to assume that the effect of our actions was also positive. The latter is tricky: As we engage our assumptions, we tend to minimize any ill will on our part and to negate the possibility that unconscious bias could be embedded in our intentions. We assume that our own intentions are positive—or at least legitimate.

As we retell ourselves the story of what took place, our tendency is to "draw data" from the action that occurred to confirm that our assumptions are correct (confirmation bias). Naturally, this is problematic: our assumptions typically are not fully accurate and are rarely complete. The problem is complexified by the reality that our intentions and the effects of others' actions on us are highly influenced by our back-stories (the diversity of experiences that comprise our person-hood and influence our current interaction). Over time, our assumptions become rooted in place. We make meaning of our encounters that drives our next encounters, not only with the person with whom we experienced conflict but with others as well. Part of the challenge in this type of situation is that the brain does not easily let go. We can begin to obsess about what occurred, blaming the other for quirks of individual personhood and for the pain the other has caused. Not only can this drive us into negative thoughts and actions against the other, but our thoughts can also turn inward, causing us to think negative thoughts about ourselves. Now we experience our personhood as being at risk.

The power of backstories

To make sense of the conflict between Lou and Ana it is also important to consider their individual backstories and their shared backstory. Together, they have a history of uncomfortable interactions with one another—at least as far as Lou is concerned. Ana's comments do not land neutrally on Lou. Instead, they are colored by Lou's history of experiences with Ana. It is also true that Lou was bullied earlier in his life because of his speech impediment. Lou has a preconditioned sensitivity around people like Ana who speak loudly and who seem to find humor in other people's weaknesses. If there was no backstory for Lou regarding Ana or regarding his speech impediment, it may have been easier to shrug off Ana's remarks. But Ana's comments do not land on neutral territory. Instead, they land in Lou's interior landscape—a place already laced with pain and fear with respect to Ana herself. We might ask, Who is responsible for Lou's pain: Ana because she should not have made her remarks, or Lou because of his unhealed backstory? In a sense, Lou and Ana are both responsible: Ana because her comments have been inappropriate, and Lou because at least a portion of his pain belongs to his unhealed backstory and not to Ana. In the end, Lou's encounter with Ana became like a strange gift to him: the depth of Lou's pain related to this brief exchange compelled Lou to be present to his own conflict history and to work at healing his backstory as never before.

But what about Ana's backstory? When I met with Lou and asked him to tell me his story, I asked: "What could be Ana's intentions that have nothing to do with you?" Over the course of my career, this has become one of the most helpful questions I have learned to ask. So often, when we are in conflict, we assume that the other's actions are about us. While on the surface this might be true, in reality the other's actions are most often about the other's backstory, even if the other is unaware that this is the case. When I asked Lou about Ana's intentions that had nothing to do with him, he did not know the answer—though he offered that he had heard that Ana struggled with self-esteem. Whether Lou is right or wrong about Ana's self-esteem is secondary. When we see the other person's intentions as about us, we become myopic in our vision and become caught in the fight, flight, or freeze response, limiting our ability to see how we could creatively respond to the situation at hand. When we regard the other person's intention through the other's backstory, it opens up our imagination—the problem is no longer just about us. This allows us to think creatively about how to respond to the situation at hand.

In a sense, there is always a "reasonable reason behind the other person's unreasonable action"—or, at least the action is "reasonable" to the actor, whether this action was taken in self-defense, to mollify the pain associated with one's hidden attachments or backstory, or out of an inclination to stumble socially. It is said that we spend the first eighteen years of our life collecting experiences that we spend the rest of our lives either sorting out or repeating (and therefore entrenching). I never did know Ana's backstory, but I guessed from both Lou's comments and his employer's comments that Ana's backstory involved experiences that caused her to become defensive when challenged and to lash out when a gentler touch would have been appropriate. Backstories are tricky because we can be unaware of how much they drive our day-to-day experiences. Backstories leak out—both in our interpretation of what has occurred and as we translate our intentions into actions. It is because of this that I often tell clients to remember the mantra "It's not about me, it's not about me, it's not about me (except the parts that are)." If I have just hit someone, then that person's reaction is at least in part about me. For the most part, however, in times of conflict, people interlace their personal histories with the drama imme- diately in front of them, at best complicating the "purity" of each party's intentions and the effect of these intentions.

The complicated nature of backstories affects our ability to work at the resolution of conflict. If someone does X (what- ever X is) and the person on the receiving end responds with X + 5,000, the receiver's +5,000 portion belongs to the receiver's backstory, and not with the original actor. The person who committed X remains responsible for that action; the person cannot, however, be responsible for the +5,000 portion of the receiver's pain. In practice, this is what makes the resolution of conflict so difficult. As we are often unaware of our hidden pain stories (or that we are attached to them), we may hold the other responsible for actions (the +5,000 part) that party did not commit. The other could go "over the top" to take responsibility, but for the receiver it may never be enough, because the receiver is unknowingly looking for healing from a problem the other did not actually commit.

Managing our assumptions

When miscommunication or intentionally poor communica- tion happens, we make meaning of our encounters with the other based on our assumptions. Often, our meaning making places us in the role of victim and the other in the role of aggressor. While we may not use these specific terms, we nonetheless experience ourselves as being on the receiving end of someone's intention to do harm, or someone's willingness to see harm where none was intended. Once we have told ourselves this narrative a few times, the story takes on the character of a grievance story, becoming cemented into place and limiting our ability to see another reality, and, given our sense of ourselves as victim, limiting our ability to find creative options for addressing our concern.

While the intent-action-effect communication model is a helpful tool for understanding how conflict develops, it is also a valuable field guide for navigating our way through tough conversations. To counteract our assumptions, we are encouraged to bring intent and effect into the public where assumptions can be clarified, and misunderstandings rectified. Practically, this might look like Lou saying to Ana, "When we met on that January morning, I experienced you as speaking loudly and disparagingly to me. I felt embarrassed in front of my colleagues. I am not saying that it was your intention to embarrass or disparage me or that you actually spoke loudly. I am describing how I experienced the conversation. I am asking that in the future, if you have a comment to make about my work, do so privately."

In real life, this is hard to do, but there are several important principles behind Lou's remarks:

1. Bringing our effect into the public means Lou is moving out of the landscape of assumptions. When we bring intent and effect into the light, we and the other party can contrast our assumptions with the other's stated experiences. Our assumptions will be challenged, and we will have more information to meaningfully inform our next steps.

2. Lou owns the impact Ana's statement has had on him. We cannot assume that the other intended to create the impact we have experienced, or that the other will recognize any less-than-pure intention on the other's part. Even if the impact of the other's actions matches the other's intention, by owning the impact as ours, we claim a type of empowerment. *If we own the impact as ours, we can do something about what we have experienced.* In this case, Lou owns the effect as his. He does not say, "*You* did this." Instead, he says, "*I* experienced this."

3. Lou does not blame Ana for the impact she has had on him. In fact, he provides a way for Ana to save face by indicating that her intent may have been different from the effect Ana's comments had on him. By doing so Lou gives Ana the benefit of the doubt, making it easier for her to recover and to buy in to his action plan for how to remedy the situation.

4. If Lou felt safe to do so, he could have provided Ana with more information, explaining why her comment affected him the way it did. In emotionally safe contexts, this extra information can help others understand why their comments affect us the way they do.

5. Lou is specific about the action that has brought him into conflict with Ana. Conflict hides behind generalizations— generalizations do harm because they are not entirely true. It would have been untrue if Lou had said, "You *always* speak loudly to me in front of others." Generalizations are also problematic because it is difficult to know what to change when generalized remarks are made. A statement such as "You are a difficult person" offers few handles regarding what to change. How does one change "difficult"? Instead, Lou is specific, giving Ana a clear understanding of what occurred—at least from Lou's point of view. This leads naturally to Lou's next gift to Ana:

6. Lou indicates what he would like to see happen next, giving Ana an actionable starting point for the change he is asking of her.

In an ideal world, those in Ana's shoes would take responsibility for their intentions. Ana might say, "I have been unkind to you. My intentions have not been pure. I am sorry." Or Ana might say, "It was not my intention to do harm, but I know that my comments have harmed you. For that I am sorry." It is, after all, appropriate to apologize for the harm of our actions even if our intention was not to do harm.

Unfortunately, we will encounter people who are unwilling or unable to apologize for the harm they have caused or for the less-than-pure intentions behind their actions. Some have never learned to apologize. Some believe that not owning their negative intentions allows them to save face. Some may lie about their intentions. And in some cases, some are unaware of their intentions or how their backstories leak through their intentions to negatively inform their actions. In defense of those who struggle with honesty about their intentions, it is difficult to know our own intentions with accuracy.

At times, we may encounter people who blame the receiver for the pain they have experienced. With Ana, they may say things like, "It was not my intention to do harm, so the harm you feel is your problem not mine." Or they may say, "You are too sensitive. Fix that." In response, there is wisdom in not being hooked by the other's accusation. Instead, with Lou, we can offer a remark like the following: "I may be too sensitive, *and* I am asking that in the future, if you have a comment to make about my work, do so privately."

It would be lovely if Ana could know and be honest about her intentions. I tell people not to get stuck trying to find agreement on the other person's intentions. It can even be difficult to find agreement on what happened—after all, both Lou and Ana will draw different data from the incident, both of them confirming their existing or emerging bias about the encounter to the degree that over time they could come to remember the incident quite differently from one another. Unless it is a court of law or an investigation, the advice is to not get stuck determining exactly what happened. Instead, wisdom is found in focusing on impact—this is the location where the lever of change is easiest to pull.

While the intent-action-effect communication model is an excellent tool for understanding our fall into conflict and for addressing conflict when it arises, it is only one door to open when addressing the conflicts in our lives. Conflicts are complex, and depending on the nature of the dispute or the character of the players in the conflict, we may find ourselves drawn to a different strategy better suited for our particular circumstance. Even in these cases, the intent-action-effect model is valuable when we debrief with ourselves after a tough experience with another person: What happened? What effect did it have on me? What defenses in me were triggered? What intention am I assuming? What could be the other person's intention that has nothing to do with me? What is my backstory? How is my backstory contributing to the impact this is having on me or on my intentions when I responded? What meaning am I making from this situation? And finally, how can I deal with this situation well?

When the intent-action-effect model is used to tackle tough conversations or for self-reflection, its guidance helps us stay grounded, to own what is ours, and to let what is the other's be the other's. This separation between what is "ours" and what is "theirs" is not about separating from the other—quite the contrary. By owning what is ours and allowing what is the other's to be the other's, it keeps the space between us clean. One could argue that the landscape of assumptions is not unlike a playfield of slings and arrows. Assumptions drive people apart from rather than toward one another. Clarifying assumptions, taking responsibility for our backstories and our intentions, owning the impact something has had on us, noticing the meaning we are making about an interaction—all of these depend on our capacity to be present to and observe what is arising within us. It also depends on our willingness to be open and curious—without judgment and assumptions—to what is arising for the other and to recognize, if nothing else, that the other, too, has a backstory that drives that person's way of being in the world.

THE NECESSITY (?) OF CONFLICT

Recently, I was listening to a radio interview with Rabbi Jonathan Sacks. Given the realities of the Holocaust and centuries of antisemitism, the interviewer asked Rabbi Sacks whether he had ever had a crisis of faith. Sacks replied, "Oh yes, I've had a crisis of faith every single day of my life. But this is not a crisis of faith in God. My crisis of faith is in humanity."[11] There have, of course, been moments of human greatness across cultures and throughout history. Just as often, however, there have been seasons of great human failure such as the Holocaust and other genocides, as well as smaller human failures such as our actions based on judgment or poorly chosen words. Our interpersonal strife and the interior condition that supports it are a microcosm of larger systemic harms within our communities and the broader geopolitical world.

With this backdrop, we might wish that conflicts would not occur at all, and that all differences remained at the level of healthy disagreement and never escalated to conflict or entrenchment. However, the best learning often emerges in the context of struggle and failure. While I do not wish for conflict, I wonder: What if conflict is also a gift to us, an opportunity to understand ourselves better, to discover empathy for others, to build deeper and more meaningful relationships? Could it be that conflict is an essential counterstroke of life, necessary for us to mature at a psychological, social, and spiritual level? While our goal is to learn how to have better disagreements, it is during times of conflict that we learn most quickly and most deeply. As the author Marcel Proust reminds us: "Illness is the most heeded of doctors. To goodness and wisdom we make only promises; pain we obey."[12] For our purposes, we can translate this quote to say that the pain of conflict is also our doctor. It awakens us to wisdom and goodness—principles to which we make promises during times of peace but that we only learn with depth in times of conflict and pain.

If conflict can be our teacher, can it also be a gateway to joy? *Could it be that when we avoid differences for fear of conflict, we also numb ourselves from life's experiences more generally, thereby also losing the capacity for deep joy?*[13] I propose that the answer to these questions is yes. There is something about conflict—or at the very least the exploration of differences—that is connected to our capacity for deep joy. Disagreeing well and attending to conflict both depend on leaning in and risking that we might get it wrong. It involves vulnerability—acknowledging both our needs and our complicity in harm. Learning to engage self and other with curiosity, to attend to our backstories and regard the other with grace even as we seek accountability for harm done . . . All of this can be messy, but, oh the freedom—even joy—that comes from leaning in. To acknowledge that we messed up or that we have been harmed invites us to hold ourselves with self-compassion.[14] It invites us to recognize that all of us fall down sometimes and that there is grace in learning how to get up again. In smaller conflicts, all of this seems possible. But is this possible in a landscape where some conflicts are so painful that even the act of breathing becomes difficult? The answer, it seems, may be discovered in finding new (or very old) ways to think about what it means to be a person and what the implications of this understanding are for our relationships with one another and with ourselves. This discovery is what the rest of this book is about.

Chapter 2

The Architecture of Selfhood and the Transformation of Conflict

If it is true—as was suggested in chapter 1—that selfhood-at-risk is a key factor in our fall from healthy disagreement into conflict, then the question of what it means to be a person is pivotal. Throughout history, people have tried to make sense of what it means to be a person, to think, to feel, and to act. Storytellers, philosophers, scientists, economists, psychologists, theologians, mystics, friends, and neighbors have all tried to explain what it means to *be*—and upon answering that, what it means to live into our *being* well. Into this mix, I offer an extended metaphor, a three-layered understanding of selfhood, as seen in figure 4, that helps us think about what it means to be a person and, by extension, how our understanding of personhood can influence what it means to be in relationship with one another. To understand this metaphor, which I refer to as the *architecture of selfhood*, we will examine each layer of selfhood—descriptive self, defended self, and deeper self—individually before sewing them back together again.

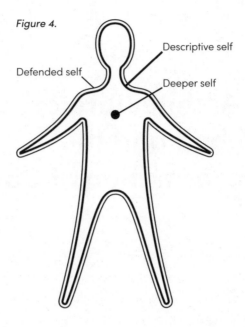

Figure 4.

Descriptive self

Defended self

Deeper self

THE ARCHITECTURE OF SELFHOOD, PART 1
Our descriptive self

Some years ago, I had the privilege of writing the eulogy for my beloved grandmother. The eulogy reviewed the frame that held my grandmother's life—the region of her birth, her family members, her connection to our family, her long trek through Europe as a refugee, a postwar start in South America followed by her life in Winnipeg, Canada. Embedded in this frame, I included bits of information and morsels of memory regarding who my grandmother was in personality and character. I tried to describe my grandmother for those mourning her in hopes that by doing so I was honoring her and the life she had led. I passed no judgment about the decisions my grandmother made in her life, her stature, or her unique way of engaging the world. I simply described and celebrated her.

Like my grandmother, we each can be described by our characteristics, our strengths, our limitations, and our life story. Some of who we are emerges over the course of our lifetime. Other parts of our identity are given to us at our birth: This is the unique "container" each of us is given to inhabit. I sometimes think of this container as our first skin or as the unique cloak we have each been given to wear. This cloak, which I call the descriptive self, includes the color of our skin and the curve of our hair, our inclinations in sport and our abilities in math, our social predispositions and the country of our birth. Our container is who we see in the mirror and, when we are honest, how we describe ourselves to others. Most crucially, *our descriptive self is neither bad nor good. It simply is.*

Our descriptive self (see figure 5) includes our characteristics, strengths, limitations, and the circumstances of our birth.

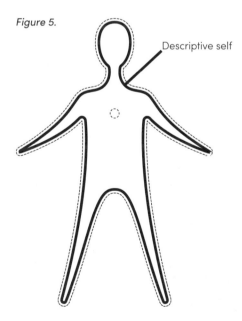

Figure 5.

Descriptive self

It also includes the foundational framework for our being: our foundational human needs, the raw ingredients of emotion and thought, and so forth. In detail, our descriptors can be described as follows:

a. Characteristics. Our characteristics include the markers of our identity that cannot easily be changed, including our race, sex, skin color, height, hair type, body shape, level of extroversion, and so on. While we can dye our hair and exercise more, our core body shape and underlying hair color do not readily change. While some characteristics change with age or can be changed with medication or surgery, the reality is that the characteristics given to us at birth are those with which we must contend throughout our lives.

Closely associated with the characteristics that cannot easily be changed are identity categories that are given to us or that we adopt over the course of our lives. Some of these can be changed with effort; others, like our identity characteristics, are given to us at birth. These are the roles we are given or take on in our families (parent, spouse, child, cousin, grandchild), the professional identities we inhabit (construction worker, nurse, doctor, educator, artist . . .), the religion (or lack thereof) into which we are born, and the religion (or lack thereof) that we choose as we become adults.

b. Strengths. All people enter life with an assortment of skills and strengths. While some skills appear entirely natural and easy for the skill bearer, other skills exist only in raw and perhaps hidden form. The collection of human strengths is diverse: Among us there are those who are skilled at handiwork, building strong social connections, growing food, or articulating complex ideas. Some carry the most radiant smile. Some are teachers, whether formally or informally; others somehow know exactly the right moment to send a text or a card to a friend in need. Some have the capacity to see humor in just about any situation; others can extract meaning from the diversity of experiences we encounter over a lifetime. All of us have strengths we bring into this world.

c. Limitations. Our limitations include our weaknesses that, despite training, will never become a central strength for us. I know, for example, that even with the best training in the world, I will never be an Olympian. Our limitations can be associated with an incapacity to attend to details, struggles in music or math, a lack of confidence in social settings, an over-inclination to regard the world through logic or emotion, the tendency to say the wrong thing, and so on. Limitations can be physical, academic, or social. Notably, these are *not* the limitations that emerge from a low self-esteem; rather these are the limitations embedded in the bodily container we each were given to inhabit at our birth.

d. Circumstances of our birth. This category includes our familial history, our mother tongue, the communities of our childhoods, and the social class of our origins. Just like the categories noted thus far, the circumstances of our birth are given to us at our birth. While we can leave our culture, social class, and family of origin, we will always bear the memory of the context into which we were born.

While a social analysis of the circumstances of our birth may argue that it is wrong that some are born into poverty and others are born into wealth, the reality remains that none of us chooses the circumstances into which we are born. The idea here is not that we cannot challenge the larger social context. Instead, the idea is that as people we are neither good nor bad, better or worse, because of the circumstances of our birth.

e. Foundational framework of our being. The foundational framework for our being includes everything from our capacity to breathe to our emotions, as well as our capacity to think and our foundational human needs. While this may seem obvious, these too are part of the container each of us has been given to wear. Our foundational needs, for example, are uniquely experienced yet common to all people and woven into the fabric of our being. These are our very real needs for *security* (whether physical, such as for food and shelter, or emotional, such as the need to be free from harm), *self-determination* (including a sense of agency or voice), *meaning* (also sometimes described as a need for purpose in one's life), *belonging* (to know we are not alone, to be cared for and loved) and *recognition* (or acknowledgment).

Similarly, each has been given the capacity to feel—this too is part of our descriptive self. Our emotions and our capacity to reason are woven into the fabric of our being. While we tend to regard some emotions negatively, such as sadness, hurt, and grief, and other emotions positively, such as happiness, joy, and humility, the reality is that emotions in and of themselves are neither good nor bad, they simply are.

Together, the five dimensions of our descriptive self create the bodily container that each of us has been given to wear. Our containers are unique, creating the distinct expression of selfhood we each come to regard as our authentic self, our personhood. Referencing the ancient Chinese philosopher Laozi, Dorothee Sölle reminds us that our descriptors are "a gift on loan to us by the universe."[1] Taken together, they are like a temporary cloak that we wear for only a season, a cloak that we are meant to care for and to use but not possess. Our descriptors are unique yet connect us to one another. It is through our descriptive selves, after all, that we meet one another, laugh, play, and make decisions.

Unfortunately, we often experience our descriptive self as separating us from the world. There appears to be a social contract that invites us to regard some characteristics, circumstances, strengths, and limitations as more acceptable, more virtuous, and more desirable than others, while other expressions of selfhood are likewise regarded as less acceptable and are denigrated. While the terms of this social contract may change from one generation to the next or from one community to the next, implicit norms are nonetheless established against which our selfhoods are measured and sorted. Therapists and contemplatives alike argue against these social contracts. Instead, they propose that *our descriptive-self containers are perfectly neutral and are neither bad nor good. They simply are.* These last two sentences bear repeating because most people I encounter do not believe these statements to be true. They worry that they are not tall enough, thin enough, smart enough; they shoulder a burden of shame because of the circumstances of their birth or their academic abilities.

To say that our containers are perfectly neutral is not to suggest that we cannot celebrate or appreciate the characteristics we have been given. Quite the opposite is true. To say that our containers are neutral is to say that one person's skill set does not make that person any more or less valuable than another person; one person's skin color is not better or worse than another person's skin color. And, as suggested earlier, to say that our containers are perfectly neutral is also not to suggest that the social injustice that leads some to be born into an abusive situation is acceptable. In contrast, the neutrality of our descriptors suggests that we are not meant to judge ourselves or others because of the circumstances of one's birth or the characteristics one is given. Those who grew up in a context of harm or on the "wrong side of the tracks" are not lesser than those born with a silver spoon in their mouths.

Unfortunately, our collective participation in the social contract that separates and divides one from the other according to the qualities of our descriptive selves means that we are complicit in this narrative. We, too, engage in judgment and endless comparisons, regarding some as better than us and others as worse than us. When this occurs, our descriptive self is vulnerable. We feel "naked" and look for masks to cover ourselves. As we regard our characteristics and compare them to those of others, we can fall into ego attachment or shame—or both at the same time. We overemphasize some characteristics—attaching our ego to the satisfaction of these characteristics, congratulating ourselves that we are not *that* which is the other—while we seek to hide other characteristics, negatively attaching ourselves to these characteristics, hoping no one sees the shame and self-hatred with which we regard ourselves.

Attachment to or shame regarding our characteristics, strengths, limitations, or the circumstances of our birth triggers a secondary attachment to another portion of our descriptive self—the foundational framework of our being. Now our emotions are on high alert; our brains begin to rationalize what has occurred; and quite likely, we grasp for one or more of our foundational human needs as we would a life saver if we were drowning. Perhaps it is our need for belonging or our need for recognition that has been triggered; perhaps we feel as though our security or self-determination is at risk. Our unmet need pulsates through our being, demanding our attention. Our needs, our thoughts, our feelings—these stand like sentinels around the descriptor that has become the primary source of our attachment, seeking to protect us and keep us upright even as they now cause us to fall headlong into our defended self.

Our defended self

Ego attachment and shame, alongside our feelings and thoughts related to our unmet needs, cause a "second skin" to grow around the descriptive self, as seen in figure 6. This new layer of selfhood, which I call the defended self, is the self we develop to hide our vulnerability. This is the place of both low self-regard and narcissistic bravado. It is both the pain stories of "Why did I blunder again?" and the over-glory moments of "Without me, this family/organization/group will never work." In fact, we can argue (as others, including Plato, using different language have done before us) that the

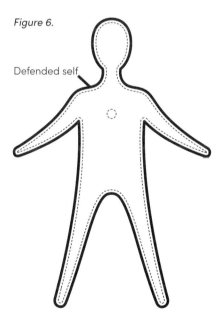

Figure 6.

Defended self

descriptive self is the face given to us before our birth (that we forget), while the defended self is the face we develop after our birth according to the roles that we occupy. It is also the face we develop when we encounter the world and the social contract that divides the world into those perceived as greater and those perceived as lesser.[2]

When I was a young mediator, I had the opportunity to work with a deeply conflicted workplace. One man in the dispute, Don, was considered to be particularly difficult. He was what some would call "a bull in a china shop." Don was strong-willed, intense, blunt, and direct, to the point of being unkind and, at times, cruel. When I met with Don for a one-on-one consultation, he showed me a much gentler and kinder face. Indeed, he became quite vulnerable. I was curious and asked him to help me understand this dissonance. Don shared with me that as a young man, others had "walked all over him." Somewhere along the way, he made a decision to no longer let this happen to him. "I flipped a switch," Don told me, "and since then, I have been this way. If I stop being aggressive now, I will go back to being walked over and I can't do that." Together, Don and I were stumped. Regardless of the direction we took the conversation, he could not undo this critical decision in his life—he had chosen aggression, and while aggression had saved him from one pain, it had created another. Don knew this, yet he could not imagine engaging with his colleagues in a more congenial fashion. Don, you could say, was imprisoned by his defended self and his internalized fear that declared that unless he put up a fight, he would continue to be lesser than.

According to the defended-self metaphor we have been developing, we might say that Don was ego-attached to his aggression and to his memory of being "walked over." Perhaps he felt an aversion to his younger self's vulnerability. Perhaps his kindness was not well received by the people in his life. Whatever the case, as Don became averse to his descriptors, he awakened a secondary ego attachment to his foundational needs for recognition, self-determination, and belonging. Over time, these diverse attachments coalesced to become a type of internalized and hidden agenda, driving his thought and behavior—all with the purpose of developing and maintaining a pain-free stasis.[3] Our attachments, after all, are not simply one-off, episodic events. Instead, our attachments become well-developed patterns, so woven into our way of being that we hardly recognize the false center they have become for us. They declare that this is how the world *must* be for us to be well.

In conversation, Don shared stories that revealed just how painful and defining his unmet needs for recognition, self-determination, and belonging had become for him. These needs, of course, are normal—each of us has these needs. For both Don and the rest of us, however, our relationship with our unmet needs creates a type of compulsion, driving us to create patterns of behavior that ensure our needs are met. In Don's case, his pattern of behavior declares that he *will* be recognized by those around him (or they will receive a tongue-lashing from him). He *will* belong. He *will* have a voice. Naturally, this brings Don not happiness but pain, even though he developed this pattern to protect himself from pain.

Don is not alone. All of us develop an attachment pattern around our vulnerabilities, including our foundational needs, to protect ourselves from harm. While these attachments can carry on in our subconscious for some time, problems arise when we encounter a triggering event. For Don, there were disagreements at work—normal, everyday disagreements—that he nonetheless experienced as though his personhood was at risk. Quite unconsciously, Don's underlying attachment pattern was awakened, his capacity for self-control shut down, and frustration erupted, causing Don to fall headlong into conflict, lashing out at his colleagues in a fashion most observers would describe as devastating. After the fact, Don experienced significant emotional turmoil and a racing internal dialogue—not about the pain he had caused, but about his life history of feeling lesser than *and* his self-justification for the way he spoke to his colleagues. Unfortunately, Don's internal dialogue only entrenched his attachment pattern. Our defended self, after all, is vulnerable to *confirmation bias*, holding the attachment pattern narrative fast, regardless of whether the narrative helps or hinders us.

Most often, it is the defended self—sometimes regarded as the false self—that we present to the world. Attached to or ashamed of our descriptors, we present to the world an over-emphasis of some characteristics and make an (often failed) attempt to hide other characteristics that we would prefer none would see or notice. Often, we do not even want others to see our ego attachment and shame, so we cover these too, adding new defended-self layers on top of the existing defended self. We don masks upon masks until multiple layers of defenses cover our descriptive self.

There is, of course, a natural beginning to our tendency toward judgment, endless comparisons, and the shift into the defended self. When a child is born, it does not appear to recognize that it and its mother are two and not one. Very early, however, the child develops a sense of its identity, separate from its mother. As the child develops and stretches itself into the cloak it has been given to wear, the child begins to regard its characteristics and recognize its skills sets, its limitations, and the circumstances of its birth. The child begins to see that it is a unique creation. Unfortunately, as the child grows and encounters the world, the awareness of uniqueness is easily paired with a need to compare itself to others. The child sees others being acknowledged for a characteristic the child does not have (or that the child has but does not see). The child's human need for recognition is now triggered, causing the child to stumble into judgment of self and other.

As the child develops into adulthood, scarcity thinking emerges. If all beauty is considered beautiful, does beauty still have meaning?[4] Beauty, one could argue, is interesting only in its narrow definition and limited availability. Similarly, if diverse athletic abilities are considered good, is athleticism still worthy of being celebrated? A healthy expression of the descriptive self dwells in abundance rather than scarcity thinking, allowing for diverse expressions of beauty and athleticism. It also encourages valuing a diversity of characteristics: One person's athleticism is not "better" than another's social ability. One person's thin figure is not "better" than another's that is round. One skin color is not better than another. This is a hard message to swallow. Even a cursory review of our self-talk, our social interactions, marketing, the media, or the historical narratives of colonialism, slavery, genocides, and other global traumas (often also including our charity) reveals how endemic our comparative and judgmental thinking is. Are we perhaps limited in our imagination, unable to imagine a world where all matter equally and where no one's characteristics are held as a liability, as a source of shame, or as a reason for self-congratulatory arrogance?

In my work, I encounter so much pain related to our defended selves—and the conflict that they create. For some, the defended self is experienced as low self-worth; for others, it is a feeling of superiority over others, both of which create complicated social dynamics; for some, it is both low self-worth and a feeling of superiority at the same time. Sometimes the defended self is expressed as denial of our basic needs, limiting our willingness to engage others. In other cases, childhood trauma places the self on perpetual high alert, ready to tackle anyone who might be perceived as a threat. The defended self can be expressed as greediness: "I must have this relationship, this job, or this promotion." It can also be seen in moments of road rage and in conflict-ridden arguments at the dinner table. Said most simply, the defended self is the person who emerges within us when we regard our selfhood as being at risk.

It is the defended self that lies at the root of racism, sexism, and every other prejudice. When a hierarchy of characteristics is established at the societal level, systemic prejudice emerges and, over time, becomes cemented in place. Now the characteristics that are considered "good" and "not good" are so unconscious as to be unnoticeable to all but those who pay close attention. The architecture of selfhood, after all, is not only an individual phenomenon. As an individual I am the bearer of a particular set of characteristics, but I also belong to multiple identity groups, each of which collectively bear a particular set of characteristics. All groups have strengths, limitations, and characteristics that define the culture and identity of the group. This idea is perhaps easiest to understand with regard to the foundational human needs housed in the descriptive self. Just as individuals have a need for belonging, recognition, self-determination, security, and meaning, so also do groups. Indeed, one could argue that injustice related to minimized belonging, recognition, self-determination, and security has propelled the Black Lives Matter movement. One can also argue that a history within white society of favoring its own foundational needs to the exclusion of the needs of others has resulted in systemic racism.

Our deeper self

The most intimate layer of our selfhood is neither the defended nor the descriptive self. Instead, it is the deeper self, sometimes also known simply as the place of one's heart, as reflected in figure 7. Together our deeper and descriptive selves form the essence of what it means to be a person. If our descriptive self is our form, then our deeper self is our formlessness, or life breath, on which identity rests. This is the house of the sacred that lives in each person. It is *the birthplace of all goodness, generosity, and grace.* In various religious traditions, the deeper self is described as the presence or breath of God, as

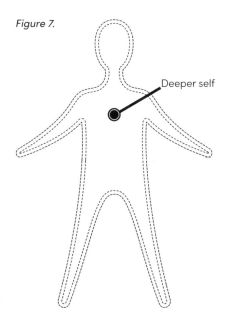

Figure 7.

Deeper self

consciousness, or as the energy of great love, coursing through the body of each person. At the place of the deeper self, we are not our past, or our future; not our strengths, or our limitations; not our thoughts or our emotions. Here, we are neither our characteristics nor the circumstances of our birth. At the place of the deeper self, we are not even our gender.

Let us think about this for a moment: There is a place within us that does not carry any of our unique characteristics that we associate with our selfhood. Here, we are not defined by the size of our income or the size of our body; we are not our social skills or our athletic ability. We are none of the awkward, thoughtless, or harmful things we have done in our lives; we are also none of our grand accomplishments, or our flights of glory. We simply are. We are breath. Or more accurately, we are carriers of divine breath coursing through us.

While our deeper self is sewn into the fabric of our being, we are not necessarily acquainted with it. Those who have traversed into this landscape often describe their first encounter with their deeper self as harrowing. We are unaccustomed to empty canvases that nonetheless pulsate with energy. Calling this energy our "true self," Thomas Merton calls this space the point of nothingness within, which when discovered becomes the beginning point of everythingness.[5] Our deeper self is the place of nothingness because it is the location at which we are emptied of every characteristic and every descriptor— including every form of the defended self—that we can apply to ourselves. It is also the place where we encounter a type of unity with a life force energy that is greater than ourselves. To find ourselves within this location is to experience a profound release. It is the beginning of everything new.

To experience an increasingly nearer relationship with the force field of life is to experience standing under a waterfall of love, to sense a beam of light cascading in and through our being. It is an encounter with eternity that has no words, though poets and philosophers alike have spent countless hours trying to verbalize it. For those for whom this idea is new, it can be a bit daunting. What do we do with such a claim? Contemplative James Finley offers the following: "Infinite love creates our hearts in such a way that only an infinite union with infinite love will do."[6] Once we have tasted this love, we yearn to find ourselves in this landscape of love once more, to receive the love that pours itself into us and over us again and again.

While the deeper self is sometimes called the image of God alive in each person, it is also the image of God alive in the "self" of each collective group. While the idea of a deeper self within a group identity is more difficult for those in individually oriented cultures to grasp, this idea is quite consistent with the testimony emerging from collectivist cultures. Groups, too, have a deeper self, a life breath that calls the group into being.

Some describe the deeper self as the truest form of our selfhood, yet—and this is a great irony—this self is not unique to any person. The most central form of our selfhood is not ours alone. It is the same love-infused, life-force energy that breathes in and through each person. The most central form of selfhood—that which calls us each beloved—is also the selfhood that beats in the heart of each group and also each person—including those with whom we might be in conflict. This means that while self and other are unique and different at the level of the descriptive self, at the level of the heart, self and other are one. In the deeper self, all judgments fall away. No social contract defines some characteristics or some people as especially good and others as shameful. No defenses divide one from the other. Self and other are simply one.

THE ARCHITECTURE OF SELFHOOD, PART 2

The face of God

When I was in my early twenties, I had an experience that, in retrospect, speaks to the idea of a deeper self, though I did not have that language then. One summer, I had the privilege of working as a pastoral intern at a downtown church in a large urban center. While I was there, a woman called the office and asked for money to tide her over until her next welfare payment. Given that most of the staff and key volunteers were away on holidays, it was up to me to respond to this woman's request. During our conversation, the woman expressed her anger at the congregation for not doing more for her, and as I was a representative of the church, she threatened to come by the church to shoot me. I deflected this comment, but I also knew I needed to visit this woman. I will confess that I was nervous.

As I boarded the subway for this visit, I prayed that, somehow, I would see God's face over the course of my meeting with this woman. I arrived, and we talked for a while. I had mostly forgotten about my prayer, when suddenly it happened. We were bent over the door of her empty fridge when she looked up at me, and there it was—the face of God radiating out from this woman toward me. I was in awe. This woman—who by the world's standards did not measure up in any way—was radiating the face of God to me.

I was still awash with this memory when I boarded the subway to come home. And then, there it was again—the face of God—this time on the face of first one subway rider, then another and another and another . . . Everywhere I turned, the face of God radiated back at me. By now, I was reeling with awe. Then an insight slowly dawned on me. If the face of God was present in that woman and in each of the subway riders, could it be that the face of God was also present in me? I had not considered this before. In that moment I felt as if I had been hit by a tsunami—of a love and an insight too great for me to grasp.

I have reflected on this experience often. What does it mean to be the bearer of God's face? What does it mean to be bowled over by a love so great that our legs become weak with the grandeur of the moment? And if we can find an answer to these first two questions, then another question naturally follows: What does it mean to practice fidelity to the face imprinted on us?

We are confronted with a mystery: we are the bearers of God's face *and* we are deeply beloved by the face that is imprinting itself on us. The writer of Luke records the words spoken to Jesus: "You are my beloved child. With you I am well pleased" (Luke 3:22, my paraphrase). What if these words are also meant for us? What if you, I, each one of us, is also God's beloved, with whom God is well pleased?

Recently, I walked with a friend, a therapist by training, who lamented, "It seems that every person has a voice inside that says, 'I am not worthy. I am not enough.'" I fear that my friend is right. At a deep, existential level, a fear grows within us that we are not worthy. It is the voice of the defended self. The fear that we are not enough goes by different names and finds expression in diverse ways. Even those who appear unaffected by emotion or are über-confident can, in fact, be displaying logic or confidence as a cover for this underlying fear. I wonder whether it is difficult for us to embrace the implications of the imprinting of God's face on us because we have not fundamentally accepted that the imprinting has actually happened. We forget that we are, each of us, made in the image of God (even when we do not operate according to the likeness of God).[7]

On that subway ride in 1991, I was bowled over by an awareness of the life breath of love flowing in and through each person on that subway car. I do not know what each person in that car had done in their lives before stepping onto the subway that day. Were there broken people among us? Those tending unseen wounds too difficult for words? Those who spoke too sharply to family members that morning? Those celebrating a joyous moment in their lives? Someone who was volatile? And yet this imprinting was on each person. We are, each of us, imprinted with the image of God, with the possibility of love potentiating itself throughout our bodies, down to our cellular structure, with a love that pours itself over us like baptism waters, a love that says to us: "You are my beloved child. With you I am well pleased." *You are my beloved child. With you I am well pleased.*

We are asked, I think, to bathe in this love. To learn slowly and over time to regard ourselves as beloved. And as that awareness takes root within us, we are invited to practice fidelity to this love, to reflect not only the image of God but also the likeness of God. This is difficult to do. And it is especially difficult when fidelity to this love invites us to see the image of God also alive in a person we have come to regard as quite unlikeable, even cruel. My proposal is that these two impulses—to know we are beloved and to see the other as beloved—are deeply intertwined. As we become aware of the first impulse, the second becomes possible.

The layers of our selfhood in relation to one another

"Both self and other are beloved." Can this be true—especially when we are in conflict with the other? Can the face of God, the love-infused energy of life, radiate in the other just as we seek to embrace it radiating in ourselves? This is the proposition of the architecture of selfhood. To understand how this becomes possible, it is important to reknit the three forms of selfhood together again. Having seen our three selves apart from one another, what is revealed when we place them back together? Like a series of Russian Matryoshka dolls, when our deeper self, our heart, is nested in our descriptive self, which is nested in our defended false self, what do we see?

Our deeper and descriptive selves need one another in order to exist. If the deeper self can be explained as formlessness, then the descriptive self is form. Just as our descriptive self (form) needs the formlessness of the deeper self to have breath, so does the deeper self (formlessness) need the form or structure of the descriptive self to have motion. Metaphorically speaking, the descriptive self is the container that *enfleshes* our deeper self. Indeed, these two selves are like strands of a double helix that connect and wrap around each other, both one and not one at the same time. Together, our deeper and descriptive selves form the essence of our selfhood.

It is said that where we begin changes everything. This is also true of the layers of our selfhood. When we root ourselves in our deeper self, a growing and stable—even joyful—relationship with our container becomes possible. Because our heart rather than our characteristics is our center, we are able to appreciate our characteristics without being attached to or ashamed of them. We are able to accept without judgment the skills and limitations we have been given—and equally importantly, we are able to accept the skills and limitations another has been given, also without judgment. This frees us to "wear" our characteristics with confidence. It also opens us to the transforming power of goodness, generosity, and grace—qualities that become more readily available to us when we are rooted in our heart center. Not only are we able to regard ourselves with goodness, generosity, and grace, but we are also able to apply these same gifts to our relationship with the other. This indeed changes everything.

Trouble arises, it seems, when we divorce our deeper and descriptive selves from one another. Our relationship with our descriptors now becomes unstable. Untethered from our heart, we place our center—our self-definition—with our descriptors. Perhaps it is our musical skill that now defines us, or our athletic ability. Perhaps it is our aptitude for logical reasoning or our ability in the garden. Perhaps it is our identity as a mother or father to which we are attached. Perhaps we are highly identified with (or averse to) one of our physical characteristics. Unfortunately, placing our center with any one of our characteristics, strengths, limitations, or needs or the circumstances of our birth functionally decenters us, making us highly vulnerable to falling headlong into our defended self.

It is profoundly difficult to regard a descriptor neutrally when that descriptor—or our defended self—is also our starting point. Without the anchor of our deeper heart self, the pull to our defended self and to judgment about our descriptors is simply too great. When we place the center of our selfhood with one or more of our characteristics, we risk associating our characteristics with the fullness of our identity. Referred to as an ego attachment, these characteristics now define us. When one of our characteristics is challenged or threatened in some way, a secondary attachment to our needs, emotions, and feelings is triggered, causing us to fall into our defended self. Now we *must* defend ourselves in order to "stay alive"—our characteristic, after all, is the center of our selfhood. Notably, we can also become attached to our defended-self reactions to our descriptors. Now our selfhood is defined not so much by our descriptors as by the patterns of self-defense that we establish to defend these descriptors.

Buddhist tradition teaches that our attachments are the root of our suffering. Our characteristics, strengths, and limitations—none of these is a problem. Appreciating our characteristics—this too is not a problem. The problem lies with our attachment to these realities. Because we must defend that to which we are attached, suffering follows—for us and for the person or group with whom we are in conflict. The Christian tradition has traditionally used the language of sin for the same idea.

When we become attached to a characteristic, we slip easily into a defensive stance. We may speak too sharply, become dismissive of another, blame or threaten the other, withdraw into self-loathing, or create logical arguments to trap the other. The diversity of ways to both suffer and cause suffering is plentiful. Recall for a moment the story in our introduction regarding Alec and Roy. Like the rest of us, both men had characteristics that they appreciated and regarded neutrally. Both men had characteristics of which they were ashamed, and both had characteristics they loved to the degree that they saw themselves as better than others because of them. Alec was attached to his identity as a calm, erudite, and somewhat detached person. Roy was averse (that is, negatively attached) to his identity as an emotional, impulsive, and non-academic person. When Alec received a promotion that Roy had hoped would go to him, Roy's aversion to his non-academic persona thrust him into his defended self. He became angry at Alec, mocked him in the lunchroom, and gossiped to his colleagues about Alec. As this occurred, Alec's calmness began to elude him. Internally, he became defensive. Externally, he leaned even more into his identity attachments, becoming even more erudite and detached to the degree that he lost the trust of the people he had been promoted to lead.

Like individuals, groups, too, are at risk of becoming attached to one or more of their descriptors, causing groups to also fall into their defended selves. Our collective defended selves have driven our global history of war, sexism, inequality, and so forth. Alarmingly, many of our attachments reside in the subconscious, meaning that while some attachments are easy to access, others (such as systemic racism) are hard to even see. Consciously or subconsciously, we may support policies that keep some groups down while lining the pockets of another group. We may disregard those among us whom we see as different or lesser than. We may look away when harm occurs against someone we regard as "other."

It may seem logical that we can become attached to characteristics that we have regarded as especially worthy and good. But, like Roy, can we also become attached to the characteristics that we dislike in ourselves? Unfortunately, yes. I can swear allegiance to myself both as better than and as lesser than. In a sense, our attachments function like an addiction. There is so much to which we can become addicted: We can be addicted to low self-esteem, the need to be loved, the need to be right, the desire to appear logical, the characteristics of which we are proud, experiences of which we are ashamed, and so on. We can be attached to our charity, or to providing preferential treatment to people who are smart or thin or who look like us. We can also become addicted to regarding the people with whom we are in conflict through the frame of "them," just as we can be addicted to placing ourselves in the frame of "us."

If our suffering is awakened by our attachment to our descriptive self, could we do away with our descriptive self altogether? Could we not simply escape to our deeper self, this landscape of perfect love? Unfortunately, this creates a new form of suffering. A deeper self without a descriptive self creates a disembodied spirituality—we fly above the world but are disconnected from its painful realities—and from the wake that we leave behind us. The famed Jewish philosopher Martin Buber, author of *I and Thou*, wrote about exactly this point when he argued against a form of mysticism that escapes from the world. As a young man, Buber was deep in the reverie of his spiritual experience when a knock at his door disturbed him. A young man was at the door, asking to speak with Buber. Eager to return to his spiritual practice, Buber sent the man away, asking him to return at another time. Not long after, the man died by suicide.[8] This event affected Buber deeply. Thereafter, he disavowed any form of spirituality that did not connect him to the real-life other. Dorothee Sölle reaches the same conclusion, arguing that any mysticism (or mindfulness/contemplation) that does not include the world and an attention to the suffering of the world is at best narcissistic and at worst dangerous.[9] While the place of the deeper self is the location of oneness between self and other, when we deny our descriptive self in our attempt to arrive at this place, we remove from ourselves all that is tangible and has form—including the other. We lose sight of the world's needs. Metaphorically speaking, while we meditate, the world burns. Practically, this means we arrive at a false expression of the deeper self, bringing neither our personhood nor the personhood of the other with us. We do well to remember that *our descriptive self—our form—is not the problem. Appreciating our form is also not the problem. Attachment to that which is form is the problem because it places our center in the wrong location, making us vulnerable to tipping into our false and defended self.*

Before we leave this section, it is important to include a caveat, a challenge to the notion of a deeper self not bound by characteristics. It can be difficult to imagine a form of our self-hood that is deeper than our descriptors. Often, our relationship with our characteristics is hard won. To finally love our characteristics is to stake a claim against all that is oppressive and judgmental. Does the deeper self undo this? Does it mean we must give this up? Moreover, how do we contend with the oneness found at the level of the deeper self when, culturally, we are told to celebrate our individuality?

Several years ago, as I was presenting this material, I was explaining the nature of the deeper self and had not yet articulated the ways the descriptive and deeper selves function together. A Black South African woman in the room said to me, "Don't take my Blackness from me." I was surprised, as I had not intended this. In her experience, however, she had observed how people have used oneness-spirituality to gloss over real and painful social differences. If we are all one, do our differences matter? If we believe that our differences do *not* matter, we risk not seeing them, and by not seeing them, we risk allowing racism and other "isms" to flourish. I thought long about this woman's remarks and revisited the architecture of selfhood. What had I missed? I realized then that the image was saying more than I was allowing it to say. In an effort to explain the different layers of our selfhood, I had held them apart. For the South African woman, however, I was running the risk of spiritualizing our unity and minimizing our differences. While this was not my intention, I revisited the model and saw more clearly that the model demands that we see and claim both the beauty of our descriptive selves, where we differ from one another, and the truth of our deeper selves, where we are one with the source of our being, with one another, and with all that is. Wisdom lies not in denying either our deeper or our descriptive selves but instead in allowing us to be both two and one at the same time. Taken together, the descriptive and deeper selves stand in protest against all that is oppressive and unjust. They celebrate each unique container while honoring the common humanity of both self and other.

Dialogue

While it is important to consider how the various forms of our selfhood interact within the same person, it is just as critical to consider how the forms of our selfhood influence our interactions with others. What does it mean to connect heart to heart with another person? How do the descriptive or defensive selves of two or more people interact?

To consider these questions, I propose we borrow some insights from the work of Martin Buber. Buber proposed that we typically engage in three forms of dialogue: genuine dialogue, technical dialogue, and monologue disguised as dialogue. While Buber did not speak about a deeper, descriptive, or defended self, his three forms of dialogue closely match the three layers of selfhood we have been considering.[10]

Buber proposes that our normal, everyday dialogue is primarily technical. Assume for a moment that you are at a social event and are meeting several new people. Your mind will likely engage in an internal running commentary of the diverse and unique characteristics of the people you meet: this person is tall, this one speaks loudly, this person uses gestures while speaking, this person seems tired, and so forth. Technical dialogue may also be applied to our understanding of nature, what we might make for dinner, or how we regard the data emerging from a scientific experiment. Applied to our selfhood metaphor, in the interpersonal realm technical conversation is defined by interactions that remain only at the level of the descriptive self. We measure, we assess—each other or the issue we are sorting out with one another—and we engage one another through the lens of our assessment. While the term *technical* sounds cold or mechanical, this is not what Buber has in mind. Instead, Buber defines technical dialogue as necessary. It allows us to regard another's characteristics, to puzzle over a task, and to determine what to make for dinner. We need technical dialogue to function, make decisions, sort out challenging issues, and attend to the necessities of life.

Problems emerge when our technical dialogue shifts into monologue disguised as dialogue. This form of dialogue includes debate that seeks to "strike home in the sharpest way" and without the speakers really "being present to each other as persons."[11] According to Buber, monologue disguised as dialogue includes people communicating only to impress one another. It can even include the talk between lovers when the focus of conversation is more on oneself than one's partner. Applied to our selfhood metaphor, monologue disguised as dialogue is the conversation that occurs at the level of our defended self. While we may believe we are talking with the other, in fact, we are talking primarily to ourselves, to our ego attachments, to our shame, and the masks we have placed on ourselves. While we may feel defensive because of what another has said, and while we may speak sharply with this other in order to make our point, when we peel back the layers of our interaction, we observe that much of what we said was, in fact, a dialogue with our wounded interior condition. We spoke more to protect our selfhood than to find a common understanding with the other.

Buber describes genuine dialogue as that which occurs when "each of the participants really has in mind the other or others in their present and particular being and turns to them with the intention of establishing a living mutual relation [between self and other]."[12] The other is neither objectified nor classified. There is a depth and an abandon associated with genuine dialogue: self and other meet as whole people. Aligned with our selfhood metaphor, genuine dialogue is the conversation that occurs between the deeper selves of self and other—but it is also more than this. Genuine dialogue is a gracious, heart-center to heart-center meeting between self and other that simultaneously makes space for one another's whole selves.

Buber notes that while many conversations begin at the level of technical dialogue, both technical dialogue and monologue disguised as dialogue can shift to include genuine dialogue. He invites us to open ourselves to genuine dialogue opportunities. Indeed, he argues that outside of relationship—and the genuine interactions that can occur there—we do not properly exist. It is in our genuine meetings with one another that we engage in an ongoing process of becoming. In a sense Buber's argument echoes the concept known in the Nguni languages as *ubuntu*, a variation of which says: "I am because you are." We do not exist outside of our relationships with one another, yet as I have written elsewhere, "the nature of our meeting determines whether we actually live and flourish as a result of our encounters with one another or whether our encounters perpetuate a truncated image of one another. While all real living is meeting not all meeting is real living."[13] While we cannot live without technical dialogue, if we live only with technical dialogue and do not grasp opportunities for genuine dialogue, we do not in fact live.

The selfhood metaphor we have been developing is not designed simply to help us understand ourselves better. Instead, its purpose is much grander. How we understand ourselves influences our interactions and our conflicts with one another. If we allow the association between Buber's three forms of dialogue and our three forms of selfhood to stand, then the location within ourselves from which we speak determines whether we meaningfully live. It also determines how well we are able to heal the conflicts in our lives.

In chapter 1, I proposed that healthy disagreements involve addressing problems as problems. We are able to stay at the level of healthy disagreement so long as one or more of the parties involved do not experience their selfhood as being at risk during the conversation. When selfhood at risk does occur, even if only in the interior condition of one of the parties, the fall from disagreement into conflict occurs. How are Buber's three forms of dialogue—and our three forms of selfhood—engaged during the shift from healthy disagreement into conflict?

Based on Buber's definitions and the selfhood metaphor, we could argue that healthy disagreement involves technical dialogue, engaging our descriptive selves only as we seek to puzzle over a problem together. While the various stages of conflict and entrenchment may involve technical dialogue, by definition they must also involve monologue as dialogue, given the close association between the defended self and our experiences of conflict. Where do the deeper self and genuine dialogue fit on our conflict escalation continuum? While short disagreements with people unknown to us can remain at the level of technical dialogue, our ongoing relationships will falter and fall into conflict if our dialogue is mostly technical in nature. As per Buber, we need genuine dialogue to exist, and our relationships need genuine dialogue to flourish. Said otherwise, while we can survive for a time on descriptive-self encounters only, if our relationships do not open space for deeper heart-center encounters, we will begin to feel less like a person. There are often no words to describe this experience other than that we know somehow that our sense of selfhood is at risk. When this occurs, we fall into conflict and our defended selves.

While we are encouraged to open ourselves to genuine dialogue during times of healthy disagreement, it is also possible to open ourselves to genuine dialogue during our conflict conversations. Mediator Lois Gold notes that our language gives us away—revealing whether we are allowing our conflict conversations to access the deeper self (or in her language, the higher self). By way of example, she proposes that mediators ask those in conflict the following question: "If you told your story without needing to prove to anyone that you are right, what would you say?" By definition, this question shifts conflict energy away from the defended self, creating space for the possibility of a genuine encounter. Gold also offers that changing single words can shift the energy of a conversation, such as asking, "How can this situation be mended (or healed)?" rather than the more common question, "How can this situation be solved?"[14] While the language of "mending" or "healing" will not resonate for all people and therefore may not always be advised, the principle behind Gold's proposal holds: Our language influences the level at which our conversations take place. Words that are technical in nature limit the conversation to the descriptive or defended self; words that are more generative open the possibility that those involved in the conversation will engage in genuine dialogue and will engage the deeper self where access to goodness, generosity, and grace becomes possible.

SELFHOOD AND THE TRANSFORMATION OF CONFLICT

This book proposes that the architecture of selfhood has something to say to us about the transformation of conflict, that how we think about our personhood determines how often we experience conflict—and what to do when conflict inevitably occurs. It appears that how well we navigate our relationship with the layers of our selfhood profoundly influences our conflict experiences.

Preexisting oneness

It is not easy to imagine ourselves at one with those with whom we are in conflict. This, however, is precisely the claim proposed by this image of our selfhood. At the level of our deeper self, we share a common identity with the other. The center of the other is also our center. It is worth sitting with this statement for a while. Can we really be one with the other—especially the one who has caused us harm? This may be easier to imagine in the smaller conflicts of our lives. For our big conflicts, this is an audacious and difficult claim, yet it is a key principle of the personhood metaphor we have been developing. What do we do with this claim? It is worth remembering that our conflicts typically take place at the level of our defended and false self—a location where we are divided from one another. In contrast, our oneness exists at the level of our heart, our deeper self. By implication, our oneness at this level means that *our differences with one another occur on a landscape of preexisting oneness.*

Before we proceed further, another caveat is necessary. Declaring that our differences occur in the context of our oneness does not mean that we obliterate our boundaries with one another. Nor does it mean that reconciliation is always possible. We will talk more about these themes later, but for now the important point is that while we can be one at the level of the deeper self, whether we continue in relationship with another person remains a matter for discernment.

To claim that our differences occur on a landscape of preexisting oneness is to remember first that the breath that courses through our body is the same breath that courses through the body of the other. The other, too, bears the marks of a deeper self, of the sacred that calls that person into being. When we allow ourselves this awareness, we find ourselves able to see the world, however briefly, from the eyes of the other. A dawning rises within us: We appreciate, perhaps for the first time, the container the other has been given to inhabit. We recognize our mutual frailness, the limitations of our bodies, our needs, and the unique characteristics that make up each person. A seed of grace falls into our heart and takes root. Now our judgment regarding the other's descriptors falls away.

As our judgment regarding the other's container falls away, we cast our vision even further, to the other's defended self. A new capacity for compassion emerges within us. We see how the other's attachments have caused a fall into the other's defended self, just as we recognize our own attachments and our own frequent falls into our defended self. All of us have fallen into the trap of becoming attached to our descriptors. And all of us have fallen—often painfully—onto the sword of our defended selves. We are not so unique after all.

Our common humanity—our shared struggle with experiencing pain and our complicity in creating pain—means that there is a type of oneness even in our false, defended self. Each of us is innocent, and each is guilty. One of the most compelling poems that speak to this reality is offered by Buddhist contemplative Thich Nhat Hanh. The poem is entitled "Call Me by My True Names." A segment of the poem is offered here:

> I am the mayfly metamorphosing on the surface of
>   the river,
> and I am the bird which, when spring comes, arrives in
>   time
> to eat the mayfly.
>
> . . .
>
> I am the child in Uganda, all skin and bones,
> my legs as thin as bamboo sticks,
> and I am the arms merchant, selling deadly weapons
>   to Uganda.
>
> . . .
>
> Please call me by my true names,
> so I can hear all my cries and laughs at once,
> so I can see that my joy and pain are one.
>
> Please call me by my true names,
> so I can wake up,
> and so the door of my heart can be left open,
> the door of compassion.[15]

We might add lines to Nhat Hanh's poem tailored to reflect our own situations: we are the people with whom we are in conflict, who perhaps struggle with their life story and their way of being in the world; and we are ourselves, perhaps longing to be free of these conflicts. In his poem Hanh proposes that there is something about waking up to our "true names"—our identity as both the one who creates harm and the one who receives harm—that opens "the door of compassion" in our hearts.[16]

Nhat Hanh's poem is provocative. Can we really embrace this reality? So much of our social construct is premised on keeping tight boundaries between those we call innocent and those we call guilty. Oh, how much we want the category of who is good and who is bad to be clear. Nhat Hanh proposes a deeper and mysterious reality that is at once both painful and hopeful. To claim our oneness with one who has done harm means we cannot use rejection of the other as a strategy for feeling better about ourselves, for assuring ourselves of our innocence. Each of us is guilty of creating harm; each of us can raise fists in protest against harm we have received. To cut off the other, to build fences between us and them, to maim those whom we call guilty—none of this will protect us from our own inclination to do harm. The poem, however, proposes that the converse is also true: a house of goodness and innocence lives inside each person, including the other, regardless of whether we can see this in real time.

If we really sit with Nhat Hanh's poem, if we allow ourselves to sink into its meaning and implications, we will see that it is not only that we cannot reject the other, or that there is goodness in self and other. In the great mystery of what it means to live and breathe and have being, a foundational and mysterious unity binds us together. Indeed, we are one. A unifying force and energy draws all of creation together, from the smallest blade of grass to the farthest reaches of the universe. All that lives, lives also in us, just as we live in all that lives. On one level, this is grand, bringing us into unity with greatness. On another level, it is humbling, bringing us into unity with both pain and harm. While the former is exhilarating, the latter drives us to compassion.

Both-and thinking

As we become centered in our deeper self and the oneness found there, we become increasingly capable, even compelled, by a both-and way of thinking. Our personhood, after all, is found in the unity of *both* our descriptive self *and* our deeper self. Further, we are *both* one with the other *and* not one with the other. In the contemplative tradition, we are *both* one with God *and* not one with God. While this may sound theoretical and esoteric, in practice something shifts within us when we become conversant in both-and ways of thinking, or said otherwise, when a both-and spirit settles into our souls. Our worldview shifts. We see that we are *both* innocent *and* complicit in the conflicts in our lives—and also in the conflicts in our world. We see that the other is *both* good *and* broken, just as we ourselves are *both* good *and* broken. We can *both* hold boundaries *and* forgive at the same time. We can *both* offer unconditional positive regard to the other *and* set limits on our engagement with the other. We can *both* engage in self-compassion *and* take responsibility for our contribution to pain. We can be *both* right *and* wrong, just as the other can be *both* right *and* wrong.

Part of what drives our capacity for both-and thinking is the awareness that in our heart space our personhood is never at risk. When we experience this type of security, we are freed to regard the fullness of our personhood with both acceptance and humility, recognizing both its grandeur and its missteps, its flights of glory and its gritty earthen existence.

Both-and thinking opens space in our hearts for the other. Recall for a moment a person with whom you have had difficult conflict, perhaps even a person you have come to actively dislike. Now, recalling that each of you is called beloved by the breath that gives you life, seek to access the love for the other coming from the breath that is also pouring love into you. *This is not easy to do.* However, if we allow ourselves to imagine the possibility of our common humanity, our oneness, we will be forced to recognize that any harm we wish on the other is fundamentally a harm we wish on ourselves. The converse is also true: the love we give the other is also the love we give ourselves.

When we are deep in conflict, it is difficult to embrace the notion that the other is also beloved. If we allow ourselves—really allow ourselves—to live in this awareness for a while, we begin to change. The most central form of our personhood and of the other's personhood is also the location of the great breath of life coursing through both that other and us. The other, like us, is deeply loved, and the other, like us, is worthy of love. While this may seem obvious, this reality is not easy to grasp in times of conflict. To claim such oneness during hard experiences makes us uneasy. We might protest: "But I am the one who was injured. Should the sanctity of my home in the house of God that lives within me not be secure?" The truth is that the sanctity of our home is secure—and it is likewise true that the other is also loved by the love that loves us. There is space, it seems, for all.

The center of identity and the "location" of conflict

As we have seen, selfhood at risk is highly correlated with the emergence (and continuance) of conflict. To transform conflict, we are reminded that the center of our identity matters. Specifically, we are encouraged to root ourselves in our deeper self to more easily navigate the judgments of others that put our selfhood at risk.

Consider for a moment a conflict between Jane and Sam. Jane, like so many women, suffers from body shame. Her friend Sam finds it amusing to make comments about Jane's body shape. On one particular occasion it becomes too much and their friendship comes to a crashing end. Who is at fault for the pain Jane experienced because of Sam's comments? Sam because he should not have made his remarks, or Jane because of her aversion to her body shape? In a sense, both Jane and Sam are responsible for this conflict—Sam because his remarks were unkind and because he judged Jane as lesser than because of one of her descriptors; and Jane because she has placed the center of her identity with her aversion to her body shape. In addition, it is likely that Sam's inclination to make comments about Jane's body has more to do with Sam's low self-esteem (another form of ego attachment) than it has to do with Jane. This, too, makes Sam guilty.

Imagine you are Jane. What are the mechanics behind the rush of pain you experience when Sam makes his remarks? The idea is simple but important: *If the point of our pain and the center of our selfhood are at the same location, we experience a conflict of interest within ourselves when we try to respond to our pain.* Said differently, if the point of our pain is about a descriptor and that descriptor is also the location where we have also placed the center of our identity, it becomes impossible to think clearly enough to know how to respond in that situation. We want to be wise and discerning, but our pain and our selfhood are so tightly bound that wisdom is difficult to access. We *must* defend ourselves. Sometimes people in conflict wisely say, "I need space to think." According to the metaphor we have been developing, taking space to think is akin to returning our identity to its home in our heart, thereby creating space between our heart and our wound and allowing us to more thoughtfully consider how we will respond to the harm we have experienced and how we will address our own complicity in the incident of harm. Being centered in our deeper self makes space for discernment, not avoidance.

Rooting oneself in the deeper self does *not* necessarily mean that Jane gives Sam a pass on his remarks. It may be that Jane discerns that she must address Sam's remarks with him. It may also be that Jane discerns that it is no longer safe or appropriate to maintain a relationship with Sam. Jane may be angry with Sam and may need time in her heart to sort out the contours of her anger and how she will use this anger well. Jane may also need the comfort of her heart center, where she knows she is cherished and loved and where she can—for herself—appreciate her characteristics as they have been given to her, without becoming averse to them.

Whatever Jane's decision is, *it is easier for Jane to discern how to respond to Sam when her center is with her deeper self rather than at the place of her pain.* From her heart center, Jane more easily accesses the principles of goodness, generosity, and grace that allow her to hold Sam in positive regard even as she considers her response to him. From her heart center, Jane remembers her common humanity with Sam, including her own social blunders. Jane also remembers her own value. Together, these impulses allow Jane to be both clear and compassionate with Sam, to honor her own needs while also remembering Sam's personhood.

While responding well to the harms people create is important, it is also true that as we spend time in our deeper self, we discover that all manner of slings and arrows bounce off us more easily because they simply become less important. Others' acts of harm say more about *their allegiance to their defended self* than it does about us. When our selfhood is grounded in the deeper self, our horizon becomes bigger and our capacity to discern what is or is not important increases, allowing us to be undistracted by at least some acts of others. Notably, when others' acts of harm do not generate a *defended-self* reaction from us, it is not unusual for them to cease the harm they are seeking to create to assuage their own defended self.

Not all harms cease as we center ourselves in our heart space. Over the course of our lives, some wounds will be so profound that it will be as though they forcefully tear us from our deeper-self center. We may try to claw our way back to our heart center, but we repeatedly slide into our pain and our defended self. When this occurs, we may need to enter the care of deeply loving souls to restore us to ourselves and to the life-breath center of our selfhood.

Unconscious bias, pain stories, and hidden attachments

Transforming conflict is especially difficult when the issues with which we are wrestling include our biases (unconscious or otherwise), our hidden attachments, and our underlying pain stories, including our trauma. It is possible, after all, that our experience of selfhood at risk is being propelled by what lies in our subconscious realm rather than by our conscious realm. How does our selfhood metaphor support us when that which is driving our conflicts is unknown to us or is only partially known to us—or when the pain story is so deeply embedded in our narrative that it is difficult to know what it means to live without this pain story?

As we make the journey home to our heart center, many of our biases, pain stories, and hidden attachments will be revealed to us. This healing work is not easy—and it is why some people resist the journey to their heart. It is difficult to release our pain, our biases, and our hidden attachments. It is also difficult to release our emotions and our thought patterns that emerged to help us sort out these challenging attachments. Because the heart center is a place of generosity, goodness, and grace, it is likely that as we return to this center, we will be confronted by the conscious and unconscious biases within us that have driven a wedge between us and those around us. To heal, we will need to attend to our complicity in the harm done by our biases. Similarly, we will be confronted by our pain stories—old and new—that keep us moored in our defended self. To make our way home, we must learn to draw breath from the source of love that beats within us rather than from the pain stories that have accumulated in our memories. Over time, we learn that our pain stories no longer define us. Love does. We breathe in and love enters our bodies with our breath. We breathe out and, by some miracle, love enters the world through our breath. The fruit of our journey home is always a grace-filled and abiding humility alongside a deep inner rest. Our healing is crucial to the work of conflict transformation. Now we walk into our differences more lightly, more able to attend to what is arising within us and less easily hooked by our ego attachments, more ready to take responsibility for our own complicity. We are now more able to be present to the other, and more able to access compassion. In a sense, we have to get ourselves *in the way* to get ourselves *out of the way*. Said differently, we must become aware of and attend to our biases and judgments in order to engage compassionately and well with those with whom we differ, and in order to be truly present to the diversity of people in our lives.

Thoughts and feelings

When we spend time in our heart center, we learn to develop a more neutral relationship with our emotions and our thought patterns. We are not our feelings, nor are we our thoughts. Yet our heart center is large: It allows us to feel the fullness of our feelings and to explore the far reaches of our thoughts without being enslaved by either thoughts or feelings. Joy, sorrow, grief—we may encounter each of these as we sort through the memory bin of our lives. Thoughts about what occurred or what should have occurred—these, too, will exert themselves as we reflect on our experiences. Rooted in our heart center, we become present to our thoughts and feelings but recall that they are only thoughts and feelings. Like a tool or an object, we can pick up our thoughts and feelings and we can put them down again. We can notice our feelings and use the information our feelings provide as a data point to help us understand the work of healing in which we are engaged. Most importantly, we recall that our feelings—and our thoughts—are not the center of our selfhood. Our heart is.

Given that our thoughts and feelings are the vehicle by which we reveal and express the conflicts in our lives, our defended self, our ego attachments, and our shame, developing a more neutral—and grounded—relationship with our thoughts and feelings is critical for the ongoing work of conflict transformation. Our feelings and our thoughts, in and of themselves, are not a problem. On the contrary, deep presence in our heart center allows us to welcome our feelings and our thoughts, to digest and release them—all without being hooked by them.

Fidelity to the deeper self and the descriptive, bodily world

As we have noted, when we are centered in our heart space, we discover a unity with the larger source of our life. This means we begin to see the world through eyes other than our own. We now see the world—and the other—through the eyes of the divine energy that breathes life into both self and other. By definition, fidelity to this deeper energy becomes fidelity to the descriptive, bodily world that includes both self and other. By implication, experiencing the world in this way means that the nearer we come to the deeper self, the more likely it is that we will feel the pain of the other, including the person with whom we are in conflict. This occurs even as we experience our own pain.

In small conflicts, it is not especially difficult to feel the pain of the other. In conflicts that feel especially harmful to our personhood, this can almost feel unfair. It would be easier somehow to feel self-justified in our negativity about the other and to remain focused on our pain rather than that of the other. Indeed, our journeys of healing will include seasons when focusing on ourselves rather than the other is critical. Nonetheless, over time, fidelity to the deeper self will always call us home again to our own sacred place of peace, from which we are also compelled to hear and see the suffering of the other, even if that other is the person with whom we have experienced conflict. It is the beginning of our compassion.

Access to goodness, generosity, and grace

Another implication of our selfhood metaphor for the transformation of conflict lies with the availability of goodness, generosity, and grace. When we seek to resolve conflict but take our restorative conversations only to the place of the descriptive self, we remain at a place of difference. Our descriptive selves, after all, are unique—they can be in competition with one another, limiting our ability to find common ground. This is especially true for our foundational needs. For example, one person's need for belonging can be in competition with another person's need for recognition. Or one party's need for security may clash with another's need for self-determination. By opening our conversation to the deeper self, we invite goodness, generosity, and grace to inform our conversation. This allows us to regard our natural differences more neutrally, to regard the other—and ourselves—with compassion. It opens our mind to curiosity and the possibility that there is more to a situation than we have thus far known. It also opens our spirit to creativity, to the imagination of what might be possible, and to the ability to see hope where earlier none was available. In short, access to our heart center allows transformation to more readily occur.

Over the years, numerous clients have asked me how they can stop their inclination to speak negatively about a colleague, friend, or family member with whom they have experienced challenges. While this seems like an easy problem to solve— just do not engage such conversations—it is much harder to put into practice, even though most of those who come to me for coaching on this topic are kindhearted people who want to live according to their values. One such woman came to me for coaching because she wanted to improve her relationship with her sister. During our conversation, my client revealed that she regularly had rancorous conversations with her friends about her sister. She also shared that to no longer engage in these conversations would be devastating for her friendships. Her friendships were premised on the struggle and the dark humor that conversations about her sister allowed. In response, I offered the following: "Go ahead, continue with conversations about your sister, as you have always done. But next time, while you are speaking about your sister, stand outside of yourself and simply watch yourself. Then, without judgment, see what happens within you." Within days, my client was on the phone with me. She could not continue to malign her sister in conversation. The act of standing outside of herself and watching herself speak negatively about her sister had awakened her.

What happened to my client on that day? One of the principles we noted earlier is that we are all deeply beloved. This is true even in our brokenness. When my client stood outside herself without judgment, she was able to remember her kindhearted nature. In a sense, the compassion with which she held herself in that moment allowed her to let go of her defended self and to return her center to her deeper self. The practice of self-compassion created a bedrock of grace that guided my client back to her deeper self, from which even more grace became available to her. My client still had real concerns with her sister that she needed to address. However, once she was able to regard herself with compassion, she was able to recommit to her core values, making it easier to know how to regard her sister with goodness, generosity, and grace.

Summary remarks

Does everyone need to understand this selfhood metaphor in order to gain access to goodness, generosity, and grace? The short answer is no. While the architecture of selfhood uses an image to describe what it means to be a person and be in relationship with one another, the principles of what it means to be a person are neither unusual nor inaccessible. Indeed, we can summarize the model's key principles as follows: (a) there is a location of goodness deep in each person, however invisible to us it might be; (b) the container we have been given to inhabit is perfectly neutral; (c) we (and that includes all of us) tend to live according to our masks, our false self—this gets us into trouble; (d) we are, each of us, deeply beloved; (e) the force that loves us is also the source that births the goodness that resides in each one of us; and (f) while we are uniquely different from one another, we are also one.

When we engage conflict with the belief that the principles noted here are true, we are enabled to see the full and complex humanity of both ourselves and the other. We also discover our own capacities for goodness, generosity, and grace, making these qualities available to us and allowing us to ground our conflict conversations in compassion. We may even find ourselves leaning into unconditional positive regard—love—for the other when by all accounts this should not be possible. Indeed, such care for the other is never "logical"—this is why it is such a mystery when it appears. The offer of love is always an experience of grace, because love for the other reflects like a mirror back on us. When we regard the other through a lens of care and compassion, we also find care and compassion for ourselves.

Chapter 3

Reflections on Selfhood

If it is true that returning to our heart promises us new life, why do we resist this journey home? Over the years, I have spoken with numerous people, friends and clients alike, who describe great pain—and yes, resistance—as they seek to extract themselves from the layers of defenses they have accumulated around their descriptive selves. After all, while we may not enjoy our troubled self-worth, we may be unable to imagine an identity without our low self-regard. Alternately, we may enjoy our positive self-image to the degree that we do not recognize how a self-congratulatory way of being is also an addiction that gets in the way of our relationships.

To understand how to peel back the layers of our defended, false self, we turn first to a traditional Swedish story:

> Because of the mishaps of her parents, a young princess named Aris must be betrothed to a fearful dragon. When the king and queen tell her, she becomes frightened for her life. But recovering her wits, she goes beyond the market to seek a wise woman, who has raised twelve children and twenty-nine grandchildren, and knows the ways of dragons and men.
>
> The wise woman tells Aris that she indeed must marry the dragon, but that there are proper ways to approach

him. She then gives instructions for the wedding night. In particular, the princess is bidden to wear ten beautiful gowns, one on top of another.

The wedding takes place. A feast is held in the palace, after which the dragon carries the princess off to his bed-chamber. When the dragon advances toward his bride, she stops him, saying that she must carefully remove her wedding attire before offering her heart to him. And he too, she adds (instructed by the wise woman), must properly remove his attire. To this he willingly agrees.

"As I take off each layer of my gown, you must also remove a layer." Then, taking off the first gown, the princess watches as the dragon sheds his outer layer of scaly armor. Though it is painful, the dragon has done this periodically before. But then the princess removes another gown, and then another. Each time the dragon finds he too must claw off a deeper layer of scales. By the fifth gown the dragon begins to weep copious tears at the pain. Yet the princess continues.

With each successive layer the dragon's skin becomes more tender and his form softens. He becomes lighter and lighter. When the princess removes her tenth gown, the dragon releases the last vestige of dragon form and emerges as a man, a fine prince whose eyes sparkle like a child's, released at last from the ancient spell of his dragon form. Princess Aris and her new husband are then left to the pleasures of their bridal chamber, to fulfill the last advice of the wise woman with twelve children and twenty-nine grandchildren.[1]

This story pairs so well with the selfhood metaphor we have been developing. The naked prince is not unlike the descriptive self we have been describing. And the multiple layers the dragon must remove bear resemblance to the layers of the defended self we take on over the course of our lives. Still, two questions remain: Why does it hurt so much to remove our defended-self layers? And how do we actually go about removing those layers?

OUR ATTACHMENT TO THE LAYERS OF OUR DEFENDED SELF

Some years ago, a client shared with me that he could neither seek the place within where he is truly worthy nor regard his characteristics neutrally. To tread the pathway to his heart would have involved the removal of simply too many scales. He could not bear the pain of even *seeing* his scales—something he had actively sought to avoid over his sixty years of life. While my client recognized that his scales seriously limited his capacity for joy, the pain of removing them was simply too much for him. Removing the scales of our defended self and our ego attachments can be described as dying before we die.[2] Our scales, after all, have come to define us.

James Finley describes the problem this way: "Imagine a bride and groom are about to be married. One week before the wedding, the groom says to his bride, 'I have something to tell you; I should have shared this long ago. I want to marry you, but I have ten girlfriends that I want to bring into the marriage with me.' Naturally, the bride is not pleased. She protests. The groom relents and offers: 'Okay, I can let seven of them go; but three I need to bring along.'"[3] According to Finley, the groom is not unlike the rest of us. Some scales we can imagine letting go. Others have become so much a part of us that we cannot imagine releasing them. And, like my client, some scales we will not or cannot even see. According to Finley, arriving in our home is like walking through a narrow gate. The false-self luggage we carry simply will not fit through the narrow gate. So we stand at the portal, unsure of what to do—let go of the luggage or close our hands ever more tightly on the handles of the bags we carry.

While the prince in our story was able to remove his layers of scales in one evening, in reality, removing our scales requires a lifetime. If the story of Aris and the prince were to continue, it is likely that after the prince's night of removing his scales, he would nonetheless be tempted in the days and months that follow to dress himself in his scales once more. After all, we can become attached to our scales. Scales did not simply appear on the body of the prince. Scales emerge to protect us from the judgments we have experienced, or imposed on ourselves, when we exposed our naked characteristics to the world. Still, the story of Aris and the prince promises joy at the end of the disrobing journey. How do we get there?

REMOVING THE LAYERS OF THE DEFENDED SELF

Several years ago, I had a dream that has stayed with me to this day. I share the dream here because it has something to say to us about our defended self and how we engage our attachments. The dream was unusual.

In my dream I came upon a soccer field and saw two teams facing off. One team was composed of mystics and saints. They glowed. The second team was clearly a group of demons. Their jerseys, if you could call them that, made them look like bats. I wanted to join the game, and I entered on the side of the mystics and saints, noticing even in my dream the wisdom of this choice. As I approached the field, I was disheartened to see that the members of my team were just stepping off for a break. (Into a dugout for a snack, actually—it was a dream.) The demon side—with a field thick with players—stayed on. Alone, I took the side of the field now emptied of mystics and saints. The game was on. I kicked the ball to the lead demon. Rather than initiating a typical play, however, the lead demon kicked the ball back at the level of my heart—hard. The demon clearly meant to do me harm. I caught the ball in my hands (I know—not allowed in soccer) and hesitated. I wasn't sure what to do. Should I kick the ball in a manner that would harm the demon back, or should I play the ball correctly? Said otherwise, should I offer judgment or grace? I chose grace. I did not kick the ball. Instead, I walked the ball over to the lead demon and kindly placed it in the demon's hands. There was a moment of peace. Then I awoke.

I pondered the dream for several days, glad I had chosen grace but left contemplating the identity of the demons against whom I had played soccer. Who were they? It took about three days of pondering for my aha moment to arrive. In retrospect, it seems so obvious: The demons were and are *my* demons. They are the quirks of personality and the addictions to my old narratives that do not serve me well.

Each of us has demons, though not everyone uses this term. Our demons can be described as our layers of scales, our ego attachments or ego aversions, our emotional programs of happiness, or simply our expectations of how things *must* be. They are our old wounds and our patterns of behavior that bind us and, in the process, harm us and those with whom we are in relationship. They are the habits of the mind and spirit that cause us to fall into judgment, negative self-talk, overbearing behavior, the need for control. Our demons also reflect our pain. Our demons do not simply materialize to taunt us. Instead, our demons emerge because of real or imagined pain, which is often so buried in our psyche we may not even know the root of the pain that defines our lives. Our demons can be loud and blaring; or they can be so well sewn into the fabric of our lives we may be unconscious of their influence. Our demons emerge from our backstories—the collection of experiences that accumulate over a lifetime and become the patterns and narratives by which we interpret new experiences—and which help define the conflicts in our lives. Our demons are also our collection of pain stories or our pain themes that repeat themselves throughout our lives.

I share the story of my soccer game with my demons because I believe it has something to say to us about how we heal our defended self, how we remove our defended-self layers:

1. Whether it is a soccer game or a wrestling match, most of us have spent nights accompanied by our demons. In fact, it appears that wrestling with our demons is a step that we *must* take in order to release our attachment to them. If we do not engage our defended self, it will control us, whether consciously or unconsciously. Herein lies a word of caution: Wrestling with our demons is not for the faint of heart. The advice given to those who open themselves to their defended self is this: Beware! You may be inundated! When a crack is opened, multiple false-self narratives can rush through. We notice our complicity in the conflicts in our lives; we observe our own embarrassing or shameful patterns; we see our biases; we lie awake, unable to sleep but also unable to get up. We find ourselves with the words in our mouths: I have seen a field of demons and they are mine.

2. There is wisdom in responding to our demons with grace rather than shame, compassion rather than violence, acceptance rather than rejection. Naturally, this is easier to do when we have grounded ourselves in our heart center. We accept our demons *by accepting the stories of our defended self without judgment and without attachment*. It can be as simple as saying without judgment in our voice, "Oh, hello, demon/defended self. There you are again." To accept our demons is to recognize them as *ours*, and to normalize them, acknowledging that our demons emerged for a reason. Perhaps they developed to

help us make sense of the world or to protect us from danger. Perhaps we developed a lack of trust from a desire not to be deceived. Perhaps a pattern that helped us survive a complex situation now no longer makes sense. Whatever the case may be, when we accept our demons, they lose their power over us.

3. When we have accepted our demons, even thanked them for the ways they have sought to protect us, we can begin to release our attachment to them. We can be assured that there are always more demons to release! Sometimes it is the same pattern that emerges again, or sometimes a new form of an old pattern presents itself to us. Or we may discover new defended-self patterns of which we were not yet aware. A friend has reminded me several times of a word of guidance he once received from his spiritual director, Sister Grace Myerjack: "The Spirit takes us back through our patterns over and over again, until we realize that they are no longer necessary."[4]

4. When we have released our demons, there is value in resting in self-compassion. Like the dragon prince, it is more often vulnerability rather than euphoria that we experience after a release of a defended-self layer. It is important to be gentle with ourselves, tender with our raw and exposed flesh. Because our defended-self layers so often reveal our complicity in conflict, it is tempting to apply new dragon scales, now of shame and self-loathing. Wisdom rests in remembering that all of us fall down and all of us have dragon scales we are working to release. Courage is learning how to hold ourselves with grace and compassion even as we learn to get up again.

ARCHETYPAL STORIES AND SELFHOOD

Wrestling with our selfhood and with our experiences of conflict is not new to our current context. Indeed, many of the stories embedded in the diversity of religious traditions explore this dynamic in one fashion or another. In a sense, these stories and the characters they portray are archetypal. We are invited to place ourselves in these stories, and to identify with these characters, in order to allow their hard-earned wisdom to speak also to us. In what follows, I offer a few reflections regarding how the model of selfhood inter-sects with two characters from the Judeo-Christian tradition: Jacob and Jesus.[5]

Jacob's night of wrestling

One archetypal character especially relevant for our study of selfhood and conflict is found in the ancient Hebrew story of Jacob. The backdrop to our story involves a conflict between twin brothers Jacob and Esau. Esau is born first and, accord-ing to tradition, is to receive the blessing reserved for eldest sons. Not content with his status as second-born, Jacob cheats his brother Esau of his birthright, not once but twice. Angry, Esau threatens to kill Jacob, and Jacob flees for fear of his life. Eventually, Jacob comes to live in a faraway land with his uncle Laban. There, over the course of many years in which Jacob and Laban swindle one another, Jacob accumulates a large family and herds of livestock. Now Jacob wants to make his way home again.

We pick up Jacob's story shortly before he is meant to meet his brother Esau. Jacob is clearly nervous. He sends ahead extravagant gifts for his brother. These gifts are not meant to say "I missed you." These gifts are meant to say "Please don't kill me." The night before he and Esau are finally to meet, Jacob and his family have one more river to cross. Jacob, it appears, is not ready. He sends his family and all he has across the river. He, however, stays back alone. The night is described as follows:

Jacob was left alone; and a man wrestled with him until daybreak. When the man saw that he did not prevail against Jacob, he struck him on the hip socket; and Jacob's hip was put out of joint as he wrestled with him. Then he said, "Let me go, for the day is breaking." But Jacob said, "I will not let you go, unless you bless me." So he said to him, "What is your name?" And he said, "Jacob." Then the man said, "You shall no longer be called Jacob, but Israel, for you have striven with God and with humans, and have prevailed." Then Jacob asked him, "Please tell me your name." But he said, "Why is it that you ask my name?" And there he blessed him. So Jacob called the place Peniel, saying, "For I have seen God face to face, and yet my life is preserved." The sun rose upon him as he passed Penuel, limping because of his hip. (Genesis 32:24-31)

I am convinced that the Jacob in our story is weary, afraid, and wracked with guilt. He wrestles because he cannot face Esau until he has come to terms with who he has been and the harm he brought to his brother.

What happened to Jacob over his night of wrestling? Understanding ancient texts can feel a bit like unraveling a riddle. If we have a key, the text pops with meaning we would otherwise not see. In this case, a key to understanding this text is found in recognizing the passage's poetic structure. The text follows an A-B-C-D-C-B-A pattern. The thesis statement, the high point of the text, is in D position, the middle.

A1: Wrestling with a man/wound
    B1: Bless me
        C1: Tell me your name
            D: My name is Jacob
        C2: You will be called Israel
    B2: Blessing
A2: Recognition of God/wound

Let us start with B1, Jacob's request for a blessing. It is not surprising that Jacob requests a blessing: he is about to meet his brother from whom he twice stole a blessing. In fact, it appears that every blessing Jacob has ever received is one that he has stolen. Now, for the first time in his life, Jacob is pleading for an honest blessing. But the wrestler does not comply with Jacob's request. Instead, the wrestler asks Jacob his name (C1). At this point, we should see Jacob wince.

The larger narrative records only one time, earlier in Jacob's life, that Jacob is asked for his name: When Jacob, pretending to be Esau, goes to their father, Isaac, who is blind, and asks for Esau's blessing. Isaac is confused and asks for Jacob's name, to which Jacob answers, "I am Esau, your firstborn" (Genesis 27:19). Now, during this long night of wrestling, the same question: "What is your name?" Jacob replies, "My name is Jacob" (D). It is a confession.

Even if Jacob had never before been asked for his name, for him to give his name in this moment is difficult. Jacob's name, after all, means "deceiver," or "crooked one." In fact, one can read Jacob's reply in passage D as saying, "I am Jacob; I am a deceiver." Note that Jacob's confession is also the high point of the story, the writer's thesis statement. The giving of his name holds the weight of the story. It is also the turning point in our story and in Jacob's life.

Instead of a blessing, Jacob receives something he did not expect, but that for him is much more important: The wrestler gives Jacob a new name, Israel (C2). The name Israel means "the father of a great nation"; it also means "straight" (as opposed to crooked, the meaning of the name Jacob).[6] Jacob has a new identity. It as though the wrestler says to Jacob, "Yes, you have been the deceiver, but you no longer need to live by that identity. I will give you a new name, a new identity." And then, almost as an afterthought, the wrestler blesses Jacob (D2).

How many of us would welcome a new name, an opportunity to release our attachments and our defended self by which we have defined ourselves? Removing the dragon scales is not easy for Jacob—it involves a long, hard night of wrestling. Nor is it easy for us. Jacob knows he needs something. But what is it that he needs? What do we need when we come to a river we are afraid to cross? The other side represents both terror and hope—terror that we might come face-to-face with the ways our scales have harmed others and ourselves; hope that, just maybe, grace might await us. We think it is a blessing we need, something that legitimates our personhood. But a blessing without confession risks being another attachment, another defended-self achievement by which we can ride above our terrors, never facing them or our complicity in the harm done. Instead, the wrestler offers us something more important: our true selfhood. This is the gift of grace we seek. Now, as dawn breaks, we are able to cross the river into our terror without fear. Our selfhood is not at risk.

With whom is Jacob actually wrestling? Through history, religious art has depicted the wrestler as an angel. But this is not borne out in the text. At the beginning of the passage (A1), the text describes Jacob wrestling with a man. Only at the end of the passage does Jacob observe that it is God with whom he has been wrestling (A2). I have come to believe that Jacob *begins* this night wrestling with *himself*.[7] How many of us have spent nights wrestling with ourselves and our own complicity in the harm done to others? Herein, I believe, we discover the great mystery of this text. In the midst of our wrestling, we discover we are not alone. The formless one takes form. In an act of great mercy, God, seeing our wrestling and our struggle, says, "I will not leave you to wrestle alone. I will stand in as your wrestling partner. I will let you wrestle with me."

The wound, which we see in both A1 and A2, is a curious addition to the text. Why is Jacob wounded? In my experience, we never come through our nights of hard wrestling unscathed. Our wounds and scars mark us and change us. We walk with a different gait after such long nights of hard labor with struggle and lament. I am convinced that our wounds can also become markers of beauty and gateways to wisdom. They remind us of our difficult night of wrestling. They also act like a warning bell that rings—perhaps with a bit of pain—when we run too far from the new name we were given in the darkness. They remind us not to stray far from the confession of our old name and from our new name, lest we fall into our old patterns of behavior once more.

Mapping Jacob's story onto the architecture of selfhood, we observe Jacob's "deceiver" identity as an expression of his defended, false self. Perhaps he had an attachment (or aversion) to his identity as a younger brother; perhaps he had become attached to the very idea of deception as a life pattern. Whatever the case may be, Jacob knew he had to release his false-self attachment, and not just to meet his brother. He had to release his attachment *for himself* so that he could come home to himself. Releasing our attachments, especially our well-practiced ones, involves nights of wrestling and confession—articulating to ourselves and sometimes to others who we have been. It also involves forgiving ourselves for who we have been. This is where shame emerges: when we have lived according to a defended-self pattern for a long time, it appears as though the pattern *is* us. While guilt says Jacob *has* deceived, shame says that Jacob *is* a deceiver. Jacob can hardly argue with this conclusion. Both his name and his actions reveal that truth. Herein we find the great lie of the defended self. While all evidence may suggest otherwise, *our defended self is not our identity*. Shame is an illusion that can unfortunately shackle us to our defended self. Like Jacob, we are not our defended-self patterns. Our "old name" does not need to define our future, just as it did not define Jacob's future.

The morning after his night of wrestling, Jacob crosses the river. He and Esau meet and have a lovely encounter with one another—even a reconciliation—before parting and going their separate ways. They promise to meet again, though the text does not reveal whether another meeting ever occurs. In fact, it appears from the text that Jacob, while promising to meet his brother again shortly, now follows a path that leads him away from Esau. Did Jacob fall into deception again, so soon after his night of wrestling? If so, Jacob's choice would not be unusual. Sometimes the pain of the past cannot be overcome, even after a meaningful reconciliation. While the reconciliation still stands, rebuilding the relationship between the parties is simply too hard given all the "water under the bridge."

Throughout the Hebrew Scriptures, people are regularly given new names to signify a change in their lives: Abram becomes Abraham, Sarai becomes Sarah, and so forth. In virtually every one of these situations, when a person receives a new name, the narrator maintains the new name for all the passages that follow. This is not the case with Jacob. The text uses both Jacob and Israel in somewhat alternating fashion. This may be for reasons of clarity, given that the descendants of Jacob also become known by Jacob's new name. It is also possible, however, that the back-and-forth nature of Jacob's name testifies to Jacob's lifelong struggle with releasing his attachment to his defended self. In this, Jacob is not alone. This, after all, is our struggle as well.

Incarnation

In the Christian tradition, with respect to selfhood and conflict, we find a second archetypal figure in the person of Jesus—especially in relation to the Christian construct of the Trinity. While this particular topic is vast and requires a much longer discourse, for our purposes here, we want to take only a brief look at this construct to understand what the person of Jesus has to say to us about selfhood and conflict.

We begin by defining the life force energy that Christians call God. Christians sometimes forget that while we often think of God as personal, God is also described as breath and as spirit. God is formlessness, not form. It is this formlessness that breathes into all persons to animate the form each has been given. Several years ago, I was attending a conference when the speaker, Richard Rohr, said the following, almost as a passing comment on his way to address another issue: "God is formlessness, Jesus is form, and the Holy Spirit is transform."[8] I was stopped in my tracks and missed most of what Rohr shared after that moment. While much of Christian culture sees God as form, the biblical narrative frequently portrays God as formlessness, not form. "Do not give God a name," the Hebrew Scriptures suggest, "lest you make God into a form you seek to control." Instead, God is described as breath, love, and the giver of life. God is also called Father and, in some cases, Mother. Indeed, there is a personal nature to the energy of God. The overriding testimony, however, is that God is more verb than noun.[9] Stated most simply, God is a life force that flows in and through the world.

Into this equation we now insert the second person of the Trinity, Jesus. Jesus is described as "form," as flesh. He was born, lived, died. Jesus is also described as both divine (formlessness) and human (form). Some attribute Jesus' designation as both human and divine to the birth narratives in Matthew and Luke, where Jesus is described as having been born of a virgin. While Jesus is not the only person in history described as having been born of a virgin, Christian spirituality has noted that there was a unique and deep connection between Jesus and God that was both profound and compelling. Jesus understood something about the larger force of life that drew others to him.

While the architecture of selfhood described earlier is intended as an extended metaphor, if we apply the selfhood metaphor to the relationship between God and Jesus, something of import emerges for us. We have already noted that the deeper self is the presence of God alive in each person, the breath of God coursing through the body that *en*fleshes it. We have also noted that the descriptive self is like the cloak each has been given to wear, the very real and neutral human characteristics each has been given to inhabit. And finally, we have observed that the descriptive and deeper selves need one another: The deeper self—breath—needs the descriptive self to have motion. The descriptive self—the bodily container each of us inhabits—needs the deeper self to have life.

If we lay the selfhood metaphor over the narrative of Jesus, what emerges is an image of Jesus as a forerunner of the mystery of God (formlessness) alive in creation (form). If it is true that the deeper self is the breath of God within us, and if it is also true that the descriptive self is our human form, then Jesus, described as both human and divine, becomes a guide who describes for us what it means to hold our deeper and descriptive self together. The incarnation of Jesus, the coming of God into the world through Jesus, is the culmination of Jesus practicing fidelity to the life breath of God (Jesus' divinity) coursing in and through his body (Jesus' humanity).

It is also an invitation for us, that we too may practice fidelity to this same breath that also breathes in and through us, and that each of us may incarnate this energy of love for the world. Herein, we encounter the third person of the Trinity, the Holy Spirit and energy of transformation. The Holy Spirit is the great alchemist, functioning as the spark that transforms formlessness and form into dynamic life and breath wherever and whenever formlessness and form meet.

Several years ago, as I was putting my then eleven-year-old son, Thomas, to bed, we talked about how God came to earth in Jesus on December 25. I told him then that God also came to the earth on March 2. Thomas replied: "No way—that's Anya's [his sister's] birthday." Then I told Thomas that God also came on August 31. Again, he couldn't believe it. He said: "No kidding—that's Stefan's [his brother's] birthday." When I told Thomas that God also came on August 18—his own birthday— he was on to me and groaned. I was not surprised when my son groaned. But I wasn't actually trying to be cute. I wanted my son to come near to what I regard as a deep theological proposition. He too bears the breath of divine life within him.

In the book of Genesis, it is said that God breathed into each person, that we are each made in the image of God, and that the breath of God is what gives us life. If this is true, then the day on which each of us was born is also a celebration of the coming of God into this world. Said differently, while Christmas is the annual celebration of the incarnation of God in Jesus, in a sense, it is also the celebration of God being born in each one of us. We also are the incarnation of God.

The architecture of selfhood proposes that Jesus shows a path to wholeness—and to care for the other—to which each is called. The biblical narrative is about *us*. Beatrice Bruteau describes the implications as follows:

It is to us that the angel of Annunciation proclaims that through the power of the Holy Spirit we will bring forth from our emptiness divine life. . . .

It is to us that the baptismal voice is addressed, saying, "You are my beloved child with whom I am well pleased." And if we really *hear* that, we will be driven into a wilderness wherein we will struggle with the question of what that means and what its implications are. And eventually we will find, as was foreshadowed at our birth, that we are lying in the manger as food for the world.[10]

Lying in the manger as food for the world is, after all, a reflection of the second portion of the great commandment: To love one's neighbor as oneself. In the grammatical construction of the passage in the gospel of Luke, the text does not say that we should love our neighbor *as much as* we love ourselves or even in the *same way as* we love ourselves. Instead, the text assumes that we love our neighbor as though our neighbor *actually is* ourselves—including the person (or group) with whom we are in conflict. Loving our neighbors as ourselves is possible because of the unity between self and other at the level of the deeper self. It is also possible because at this same place, unity with God invites us—no, compels us—to see the world and its pain through God's eyes. And finally, it is possible because when we are rooted in our deeper self, we release our inclination to become addicted or attached to descriptive-self characteristics. We become stabilized in the container we have been given to inhabit, and we learn to embrace—even delight in—our first skin, even as we lose our inclination to judge others, alienating ourselves from them.[11]

Chapter 4

Conflict Transformation

In early 2020, I bought the cookbook *Salt, Fat, Acid, Heat*.[1] I enjoy cooking, and I thoroughly enjoyed this book. One principle reinforced in this book is the importance of "salting from the inside." By adding salt early in the cooking process, salt can seep deep into a dish's ingredients. When this happens, the food is more flavorful, and the amount of salt needed is less than when salting occurs only "from the outside."

"Salting from the inside" is an excellent image for managing and transforming conflict—and for accessing the deeper self when in conflict. If we salt only from the outside—that is, if we only learn the skills of conflict transformation without also transforming our interior condition—it is difficult to actually apply these skills when the moment to do so emerges, and we quickly burn out. The skills we have learned will not be aligned with our interior condition, and as a result they will be unsustainable. It is like trying to grow a tree without roots. Of course, every one of us sometimes slides into the myriad ways of doing it "wrong." And there are situations that are so challenging, it is hard to know what it looks like to manage conflict correctly: even if one were to do it perfectly right, it is impossible to avoid the creation of pain. Nonetheless, it is possible to limit the slide into doing it wrong. This chapter allows us to imagine several avenues for transforming situations of conflict. While several practical skills are included, each is grounded in the principle of salting from the inside—transforming our interior condition in hopes that we might have a chance to engage with conflict relatively well.

OUR INTERIOR CONDITION AND UNCONDITIONAL POSITIVE REGARD

In 2012, I was reading the book *Theory U*, when I came across the following quote by CEO William O'Brien: "The success of an intervention depends on the interior condition of the intervenor."[2] O'Brien's quote stopped me in my tracks—or more accurately, it stopped me in my reading. I reread it several times. Intuitively, I knew that O'Brien was right—indeed I had already suspected this. But I had never before heard this idea articulated this way. Granted, the success of an intervention is about more than one's own interior condition, and one can take too much responsibility for a project's success, ironically limiting the project's success (though this also reflects one's interior condition)! Still, whenever we deal with conflict, each one of us is also an intervenor. And for each one of us, one's interior condition matters.

Several years ago, I was mediating a dispute between the leader of a start-up company and his two key investors. The start-up had begun promisingly enough, but within nine months the project showed signs of struggle. The key investors tried to provide guidance and support; the more they tried, however, the more their support was rebuffed. Instead, the start-up leader became angry with and abusive to his investors. Eventually, the project crashed altogether. About six months later, the three parties requested mediation. Their goal? To be able to pass one another on the street without needing to cross to the other side. None of the three parties wanted to resurrect the business, nor did they wish to recoup their losses. Instead, the parties wanted to continue living comfortably in the small town all three called home.

After an interview and coaching session with each party, we proceeded to mediation. The two investors behaved beautifully. They were gracious and gentle in their honesty. They gave the start-up leader the benefit of the doubt; they offered him multiple ways to save face; they spoke their truth with kindness. And they shared their hopes that they could pass each other on the street without needing to cross to the other side. The start-up leader was everything the investors were not. He rolled his eyes, threw down his pen, stomped his feet, made snide remarks, and distorted what had occurred. Where the investors were gracious, he was hostile; where the investors spoke their truth with kindness, he shared his truth harshly. As I facilitated this session, it would have been easy for me to fall into judgment against the start-up leader. Instead, O'Brien's words rang in my ears: *The success of an intervention depends on your interior condition.* I knew that if I sat in judgment over the start-up leader, I would give the investors permission to do the same. Even if my questions were perfectly phrased, an interior condition of judgment and disregard would leak out, as if through my pores, making it even more difficult for the start-up leader to find his voice of generosity and grace.

And so, I leaned on one of the underlying core principles of conflict transformation that salts from the inside: *unconditional positive regard*—or if you prefer, unconditional love. The famed American psychologist Carl Rogers noted that if he regarded people with judgment, they resisted his care and nothing therapeutic could be accomplished between them. If he regarded people with unconditional positive regard, they felt accepted and healing could begin. The same holds true for our encounters with others in times of discomfort, disagreement, or conflict. When we regard the person with whom we are in conflict with unconditional positive regard, we open ourselves to seeing the humanity of the other, allowing for a transformational encounter with the other to occur. This commitment does *not* mean we cannot hold others accountable or share our truth with another person—however, when we invite accountability or share our truth through the lens of unconditional positive regard, the potential for a transformational encounter is significantly enhanced.

In the case of the start-up leader and the two investors, I absolutely needed to hold all three accountable to the guidelines to which each had committed at the start of the mediation process. While this was easy to accomplish with the investors, it was trickier with the start-up leader. As we talked, I kept a voice running in my head: *I love this person unconditionally. I care for this person unconditionally.* And, sometimes with desperation: *God! Help me love this person unconditionally!* As the voice in my head tended to my interior condition, I spoke kindly but firmly with the start-up leader. I summarized key points to ensure the parties had the greatest chance of understanding one another. I reminded the leader of the guidelines. I called for a break so I could speak individually with the start-up leader (and then the investors). In the end, I sent both parties home before the session was meant to finish. After the meeting, I coached each party individually. A few weeks later, we met for a second mediated conversation. Now the start-up leader was ready. He contributed well to the second session, allowing us to achieve the goal each had stated at the beginning: to be able to pass one another on the street without needing to cross to the other side.

To salt ourselves from the inside is to learn the discipline of unconditional positive regard. Indeed, one of the hardest questions I have posed to leaders is this: "Do you love the people you are leading?" I ask this of church leaders and business leaders alike (though I modify the language to fit the context). If the leader offers an unreflective yes, we talk further to determine the depth of this yes. If the leader says no, I say that we need to talk, because a lack of positive regard for the people we lead (read: the people we serve) will leak out of us. Our people (or our clients) will recognize our spirit of judgment, limiting our capacity to "successfully intervene." The practice of unconditional positive regard does not mean we cannot hold people accountable. Instead, it reflects the commitment to value the personhood of every person we encounter, regardless of the harm that person may cause or has caused others or ourselves. In practice, this is not easy to do. Unconditional positive regard depends on holding the other's personhood separate from the actions the other may have done. The humanity of the other (and our own humanity) is not the same as the actions either of us has taken. We are not good because we have done a good action, nor are we bad because we have done a bad action. Our actions do not determine our inherent value or our inherent goodness as persons.

In one of the workshops I teach, at the start of the second day I invite participants to recall to their minds a person with whom they have had significant tension (though this need not be the person with whom they have experienced the most difficulty). Notice, I do not call the person they are to visualize "a difficult person." To do so would be to label the personhood of the other as "difficult," causing us to tip over into judgment and our defended self, possibly inviting a shame response on the part of the other. Instead, the assignment's phrasing focuses on describing the other as "someone with whom you have experienced difficulty or tension." Once participants identify their person, I invite them to regard the other through a lens of unconditional positive regard. (In principle, this assignment could be modified to visualize oneself as the object of unconditional positive regard.) In this exercise, we are not visualizing a conversation, we are not reciting our list of woes, nor are we imagining what peace with the other could look like. We are simply holding the other in our consciousness in a spirit of grace. After a few minutes of silence, we release ourselves from this visualization, and after some debriefing, we return our minds to the workshop agenda. I am not proposing that this small visualizing exercise changes the world; I am proposing, however, that this exercise deepens our capacity for unconditional positive regard, and by extension transforms our relationships with one another.

The principle of each person's inherent value and goodness has significant implications. It means, for instance, that we can offer unconditional positive regard for another's personhood, even as we invite accountability for harmful actions the other has taken. While this is challenging, even more challenging is the corollary implication: we can view *ourselves* with unconditional positive regard, even as we accept accountability for the harmful actions we have taken. Salting from the inside and learning to positively regard the personhood of the other is a lifelong journey. One never "arrives." But the getting there promises to be significantly more joy-filled when we are properly salted.

PRINCIPLES FOR MANAGING CONFLICT

When I was about nineteen years old, I went to see a movie with a friend in downtown Winnipeg, where I grew up and where I was living at the time. After the movie was over, my friend and I waited for the bus to take us home. There were about ten people in line at the bus stop. I was the last person in line. Suddenly, a man came running toward us from an alley across the street. The man was Indigenous, and as he crossed the street he began yelling, "You white people; you stole our land." The man yelled at each person in the bus stop line, beginning with the person at the front of the line and ending with me. Some people turned their backs on the man; some people yelled back. As the tenth person in line, I had a few moments to think. When he came to me, I said, "You're right. And I'm sorry." The man turned the corner and ran away—or so I thought. About two minutes later the man was back—but this time, just for me. He planted his feet in front of me and looked me in the eyes. I was nervous. Then, quite gently, he said to me, "Thank you." And he walked away.

I was stunned by this experience, and profoundly humbled. I share this story here because in this very short encounter—in total, it lasted maybe sixty seconds—so much about the nature of conflict is revealed. For example:

1. *Time helps.* When conflict takes us by surprise, we are not typically at our best. Because I was the last person in line, I had a few seconds to think. This gave me just enough space to be reflective in my response. Taking time to think carefully about the situation and our response to it can help us be better at dealing with conflict.

2. *Preparation matters.* Because by the time of this encounter I had spent several years already thinking about issues of justice, land title, and immigration, I could readily agree with this man. In a sense, I was prepared for this interaction. While we cannot be prepared for every situation that arises, many conflicts in our lives represent repeat performances. We

encounter the same (or similar) events again and again. Often, we respond to each event in the same fashion as before, with devastatingly similar results. Being prepared for conflicts that will emerge and preparing for an appropriate response is a gift we give both ourselves and others. Doing so allows us to be thoughtful in our response even when surprise encounters occur.

3. *Thoughtful responses level the playing field.* When we experience conflict, our temptation can be to fight back, turn away, or freeze in place (known commonly as the fight, flight, or freeze response). But a thoughtful response has the potential to change the dynamic between us and the other person. A thoughtful response is both kind and honest. After all, if we are only kind, we are permissive; if we are only honest, we are brutal. A response that is both kind and honest upholds our humanity and that of the other person. By being honest, we honor our experience; by being kind, we remember to regard the person with whom we are in conflict with dignity and grace. In my encounter with this man, "You're right" is an honest response—it recognizes the truth in the man's story. "I'm sorry" is a kind response—it engages the speaker with dignity.

4. *Each of us has a need to be seen and heard.* When we genuinely see and hear another person, we honor that person's human need for recognition. What surprised me about my interaction with the man at the bus stop was how I also felt seen by him and, as a result, how I felt somehow more human after our exchange. When the man returned to say thank you, I felt honored. I hope he felt the same with my response to him. In conflict, when we genuinely hear and see another person, we honor that person's humanity. In fact, if conflict robs us of some of our humanity, hearing and seeing the other person gives both of us some of our humanity back.

5. Each person is climbing a mountain. When I was a young adult, a friend shared the following quote with me: *Be gracious with each person that you meet; each person is climbing a mountain.* I do not know what that man's mountain was on that particular day (though the history of systemic injustice against Indigenous people is enough of a daily mountain to climb), nor did he know the mountain I may have been climbing at that moment. Nonetheless, when we begin an interaction with the assumption that the other person has no mountain to climb, we are inclined to take things more personally than they are intended, limiting our ability to be thoughtful in our response. Conversely, when we assume the other person is climbing a mountain, we begin our conversations with a spirit already primed with grace.

6. A little emotional distance is helpful. Perhaps because I did not *feel* Canadian until I left home at eighteen years of age (my parents immigrated to Canada as adults), I was able to regard issues of land title and justice for Indigenous people with a bit of emotional distance. It is possible that this distance allowed the words "You're right and I'm sorry" to roll more easily off my tongue. Without some emotional distance, we readily experience our personhood as being at risk when conflict occurs. We become defensive, limiting our ability to hear the truth in the other person's message to us. Just a little bit of distance allows us to see the conflict in its larger context, remembering that while we may be involved in the conflict, the other person's complaint does not need to threaten our personhood.

7. Too much emotional distance is a problem. Too much emotional distance says that nothing touches me, and nothing is my responsibility to fix. It also says that the other person's concerns are not my responsibility. While I personally did not steal Indigenous land, I benefit every day from the land that was taken. In conflict, we must nurture the capacity not only for appropriate levels of emotional distance but also for appropriate levels of emotional connection. When this is in place, we can hear the complaint the other has with us—and we can respond to this complaint—without becoming resistant to the perspective we are being asked to hear.

8. *Find the yes-able statement.* Years ago, I was crossing the border into the United States when the border guard, knowing the type of work I do, asked me for one piece of wisdom that would help him de-escalate grumpy colleagues and angry travelers. I responded by encouraging him to look for the "yes-able statement." Yes-ables are those ideas or emotions in the other person's concerns to which we can readily say yes. In the case of my interaction with the Indigenous man, he was and remains correct in his complaint. White people have stolen Indigenous land. While it is unlikely that those of us at the bus stop physically took Indigenous land, it remains true that white people continue to benefit from this theft even as Indigenous people continue to suffer losses associated with this theft. Yes-ables honor the truth in the other person's story. Yes-ables can be about facts with which we agree; or they can be about the other person's feeling and emotion. In other words, even though I may be unable to say, "I agree with your opinion regarding X," I will likely be able to say, "I can tell that this has had a huge impact on you." In my experience, offering a yes-able statement is one of the quickest ways to de-escalate conflict. The yes-able also, very practically, offers dignity to the other party by communicating our commitment to hearing and honoring the truth in whatever it is that the other has shared.

9. *Honor the kernel of wisdom in each person.* I have been continually amazed in my work with how much I learn from

even the grumpiest conflict participants. When I begin with the assumption that each person's perspective carries a kernel of truth, I listen differently, and I hear differently. Truth is revealed to me that I otherwise would have missed.

10. Practice unconditional positive regard. While I did not have the language of "unconditional positive regard" on that evening at the bus stop, I am convinced that a commitment to seeing the full humanity of the other creates a strong foundation upon which differences can be meaningfully explored.

FORGIVENESS

I have been teaching about forgiveness for well over twenty years. In this time, I have noticed how the publicly accepted definition of forgiveness has gradually changed. Earlier, at least some workshop participants regarded forgiveness as something we give to the other. It was the equivalent of saying "It's okay" and was closely associated with reconciliation, of restoring self and other to one another. Today, virtually all workshop participants regard forgiveness first and foremost as something we give to ourselves. It is about releasing the power that an incident (or series of incidents) has over *us*. Forgiveness is a form of "letting go," though the word *forgiveness* gives the idea of letting go an important heft that the words *letting go* cannot achieve. Forgiveness is a weighty, even sacred, act.

With forgiveness, we release our attachment and our aversion to so much: the original incident; the way our memory of the original incident has enslaved us and continues to cause us pain; our desire for retribution; the grievance story that we have developed that helps us explain what happened; the pain this incident has created in our lives; the ways the conflict has become a source of identity for us; our feelings of complicity, guilt, and shame; our right to feel sorry for ourselves; and likely more. In cases of extreme harm, forgiveness even asks us to release our attachment to a perfect justice, or a healed outcome. In these cases, no act of justice, whether restorative or not, can ever fully repair the harm that was done. Forgiveness presents itself to us like a mystery: It is in release that we find ourselves again. It is in letting go that we find solid ground. As we release one attachment after another, a pathway is channeled from our defended self back to our heart, allowing us to experience our full and grounded personhood once more.

Some who have walked the journey of forgiveness describe feeling free, feeling that they are themselves again, as though they have returned to the land of the living. Some describe spiritual experiences, sensing light cascade like a waterfall over them, and being bowled over by a love of and for God, the giver of life. Forgiveness in these moments is an experience of oneness, cohesion. Of course, sometimes forgiveness is not like this at all. Sometimes forgiveness is simply hard work, more a rational commitment than a spiritual experience. In these cases, forgiveness is a daily—perhaps even hourly—commitment to releasing one's attachments to the pain in one's life.

Whether our forgiveness journey is exhilarating, plodding, or just hard work, our experience of forgiveness will provide us with an interesting puzzle: While forgiveness may be for the self, by channeling us back to our deeper self, forgiveness becomes about the other as well. The deeper self, after all, is also the place where self and other are one. And so, as we return to our deeper self, as we forgive and release our attachments—even if only for our own mental health and well-being—we find ourselves in the midst of a strange experience. At home in our deeper self, we encounter the presence of the other. While we may have pursued forgiveness for our own well-being, now we are confronted with the reality of the other. We may pause. We may stumble. Can we tolerate being in the same space as this person? Is this person worthy of the deeper self, the heart center where self and other are one and where divine energy resides?

And so we encounter yet another attachment we must relinquish—the desire that the deeper self space be ours alone—or at the very least, that it be reserved for us and the people we love. Forgiveness asks so much from us. Can it ask us to release even this? If we allow ourselves this release, a second expression of forgiveness may arise within us: we see the other with eyes of compassion. When we fully enter the deeper-self center and the sacred space it creates, we discover a type of freedom: We are no longer hooked by the other's broken form, attachments, or false self. We regard the other with neither judgment nor fear. The other's deeper self now comes into focus *even if we cannot see it in real time*. A strange feeling comes over us as we become aware of the unity that binds us, self and other, together, even in the context of a painful and broken relationship. Planted on the common ground of our deeper selves, we begin to see one another's full selves. We see each, self and other, as both good and not so good; neither above the other; each having, over the course of life, created harm and each having been harmed by others. We see that which is broken, yes—but we also see that which is beautiful. In short, we see the fullness of our shared and common humanity with the other.

Our shared humanity leads naturally to a third expression of forgiveness: extending a hand of grace, in some form, to the other. Some may worry that the third expression of forgiveness lets people off the hook. In truth, forgiveness does quite the opposite: forgiveness confirms that harm was done (otherwise there would be nothing to forgive). While extending a hand of grace can be as simple as wishing the other well, it can also include overtures of care and compassion for the other. In some cases, this stage of forgiveness opens the door to reconciliation; at other times for reasons of emotional or physical safety, it includes holding boundaries with the other but in a manner that is neither derisive nor unkind.

Some years ago, a friend undertook a forgiveness exercise: She made a list of all the people she wanted to forgive and over a period of weeks, actively forgave each person. One by one, she called each person to her mind. Then she repeated the words, "I forgive you for the harm you have caused me. I ask for forgiveness for the harm I caused you. I release both you and me from our common story of pain." For some people, it seemed enough to say these sentences only once. For others, my friend felt the need to repeat these phrases for several days. And in still other cases, my friend followed up in person with those to whom she was offering forgiveness and also offered an apology. While in most cases my friend had a sense that her offers of forgiveness "took," there was one person whom my friend sensed could receive neither her forgiveness nor her apology. My friend was puzzled. In conversation, my friend and I agreed that there are times in our relationships when we place our gifts of confession and forgiveness onto the middle of the bridge that spans the space between us and another. We may wait for the other person to receive the gift. If the other person does not come, we have permission to leave the gift on the bridge and return to our lives. When ready, the other person will come to the bridge to find the gift.

Nonviolent nonresistance to ourselves
Several years ago, I was walking with a friend through the hills of Spain along the Camino pathway when the conversation

between us ventured into the hard topic of forgiveness. "How do you forgive someone who has deeply harmed you," my friend asked, "especially when the other person takes no responsibility for the harm they have done?" As we talked, my friend complexified the discussion by adding an additional challenge: "Okay, but how do you forgive someone when— for your own protection—you must draw clear boundaries between yourself and the other person? Is forgiveness possible in such an environment?" To concretize the dilemma, my friend and I exchanged stories of complicated forgiveness scenarios of which we were both aware: a sister seriously harmed by a brother; a friend publicly maligned by a family member; a client suffering a "death by a thousand cuts." In each of the stories we shared, the people wrestling with forgiveness faced situations where, in the absence of hard boundaries, the risk of being harmed by the other continued. How does one maintain hard boundaries (such as telling a brother that he may not visit) and still forgive the other?

In the situations my friend and I discussed, the people wrestling with forgiveness also wrestled with guilt because of their dislike for the offender, and with shame because of their inability to forgive. They struggled with an unattainable image of what a "good" person is—an image to which they were held by those around them despite the unreachable nature of their goal. Some of those wrestling with forgiveness struggled with a desire for vengeance, a desire for harm to come to the person who had harmed them. As my friend and I puzzled over these questions together, I proposed that part of the answer to the conundrum of forgiveness must lie in the practice of nonviolent nonresistance to *oneself*.

The practice of nonviolent nonresistance to ourselves allows us to receive our feelings of shame and dislike—even vengeance—*without judgment*. We accept that these feelings exist and that these, in fact, *are* our feelings. When we acknowledge our feelings and regard them without judgment, we experience neither attachment nor aversion to our feelings; we neither wallow in nor deny them. The feelings are simply feelings. We may even thank our feelings for the ways they have sought to protect us. When this occurs, we are no longer bound by our feelings. We can now much more neutrally engage the question of how to respond to those who have harmed us.

In contrast, too often we practice a resistant response to our feelings—and our demons—entrenching our pain and the delusions we create for ourselves to protect us from our feelings. We resist our feelings, possibly denying that they exist. What we do not see (or choose not to see) becomes like a sinkhole. We fall easily into this hole even as we are unaware or deny that this hole exists. Quite simply, we are more likely to be bound by something we cannot see than by something we can see. Alternately, we may recognize our feelings but respond by becoming violent with ourselves about these feelings—self-flagellating in hopes that doing so will cause us to behave more like the image we have of who we should be. Or we may become consumed by our feelings to the degree that we *are* our feelings. Our feelings, we could say, have become an attachment, a ball and chain around our lives, limiting our freedom. Both self-flagellation and being consumed by our feelings mean that the *only* thing we see is the sinkhole in our lives. When this occurs, we will also fall in.

Nonviolent nonresistance to ourselves allows us to receive ourselves in our wholeness—our deeper self, descriptive self, and defended self. It allows us to practice self-compassion for the wholeness of who we are. By accepting our feelings and our demons without judgment, it allows us to release these feelings, returning us to our deeper-and-descriptive self identity. It also allows us to reestablish within us the capacity to see the full self of the other—a key ingredient for forgiveness. In conflict, it is easy to see the other's defended self. Seeing the other's deeper and descriptive selves in a neutral fashion is much more difficult. When we receive ourselves in our wholeness, we are much more able to practice nonviolent nonresistance to the wholeness of the other—inclusive of the other's deeper and descriptive selves When this happens, forgiveness becomes possible. After all, none of us is innocent of the fall into the defended self.

Forgiveness, boundaries, and reconciliation

But what about my friend's question? Is it possible to forgive and hold boundaries at the same time? The need for accountability and the need to hold boundaries with the other naturally complicate forgiveness, as it has a way of reawakening to one's mind the original harm that caused the need for enhanced boundaries in the first place. Without heartfelt encounters with one another, it is also easy to misunderstand one another, risking a turn away from forgiveness and back into conflict once more. What options do those in this situation have? In times such as these, forgiveness is not so much a one-time event as it is an ongoing decision that is made fresh each time the boundary with the other is reset. It involves a dogged commitment to recalling both one's own deeper self and the deeper self of the other. And when we have the inner fortitude to do so, remembering that on another plane, self and other are also one.

For forgiveness and boundaries, it is also critical to remember that forgiveness and reconciliation, while related, are not the same. While reconciliation depends on forgiveness, forgiveness does not require reconciliation. Reconciliation involves a truly restored relationship where, after conflict, self and other are at ease with one another once more—even, at times, to the degree that the relationship is strengthened and deepened because of the reconciliation experience. Naturally, it is difficult to truly reconcile in the absence of forgiveness. And even if the parties have forgiven, it is also often difficult to reconcile when one or both parties take little or no responsibility for the harm they have done. In other cases, the parties have taken responsibility and have forgiven one another but are nonetheless not yet ready to reconcile. The journey back to one another simply takes time.

It is common to desire a reconciliation in situations of conflict in order to be at peace with one another once more. It is especially common for those watching from the sidelines to expect this from those in conflict or those who have forgiven. Nonetheless, for reasons of emotional or physical safety, there are situations where reconciliation is neither appropriate nor safe. In situations like these, those involved may end their relationship altogether or may keep their relationship at a safe emotional distance. In other cases, a limited reconciliation may be possible but still under the constraints of tightly held boundaries. In these cases, it may be important for third parties to be present at each encounter, and if conversations do take place, for them to remain at a level where the parties can easily find breath and escape when the need to do so emerges. There are, of course, situations where full reconciliation does take place. When this occurs, ease returns to once-broken relationships. Love and joy now flow freely in the once-thorny space between self and other.

Compassion and grace

One of the challenges associated with forgiveness is that grace for the other is possible only when we have practiced grace for ourselves. I am not speaking here of get-yourself-off-the-hook grace, which means we are responsible for nothing. Instead, it is the grace that emerges from a long and hard look at ourselves, recognizing our own complicity in the complex conflict and social dynamics in which we are involved. An honest self-assessment will assure us of our frailty! Wisdom is found not in self-flagellation but in embracing ourselves with care, remembering to love ourselves unconditionally. When we practice self-compassion, we develop a spirit of holy tenderness within ourselves, creating a larger landscape of compassion within our souls. Resting in this landscape, we find ourselves surprised by what we thought was not possible: We discover an internal inclination to also regard the other with compassion. Our prior assessment of the other had already convinced us of the other's complicity. Now, buttressed by our compassionate inner environment, we are assured not only of the other's complicity but also of the other's frailty: the other, like us, is human, fallible and broken. And, with humility, we discover that the spark of the divine also lives in the other, just as it lives in us.

In practice, arriving at this kind of grace is difficult to do. It takes incredible courage to hold the other with compassion after we have been harmed—especially when the other avoids responsibility for harm done. A deep inner strength is required to offer grace and to invite accountability at the same time. It is a feat of bravery to commit to compassion and grace while knowing that in some cases, our compassion will never be matched by the other person's ability to take responsibility for the part the other has played—either because the harm done is too great or because the other person is unwilling, unable, or not ready to take responsibility. In these cases, grace is sometimes partnered with our willingness to lay down our right to defend ourselves, to be right, and to have our story fairly heard—at least by the other party.

When I teach this material, people often ask, "But—can't we hold the other person accountable? Does grace not give the other permission to continue to do harm?" In my experience the opposite is true. When we touch the heartbeat of grace, we finally know how and for what we must hold the other accountable. Until grace happens, our exercises in accountability are too often marked with bias and a desire for vengeance—even if cloaked in kind language. When we regard the other's full humanity, we can speak to or about the other in a manner that invites accountability rather than wielding accountability over the other like a hammer.

Part of the difficulty with bias-laced accountability is that it dances with the dynamic of scapegoating. We often use the word *scapegoat* to describe someone who is unjustly accused of harm done. However, the word and its implications have a much broader meaning. In ancient Judaism, once a year a goat was brought into the community. The people placed their individual and collective sins onto the goat and chased the escaping goat out of the community. While there was surely value in this exercise, scapegoating today can mean we do not need to look at the brokenness within ourselves. If we declare the other a villain, we place the category of "bad" onto the other, reserving the category of "good" for ourselves. With time, we place increasingly more people into the category of "bad" in order to protect our own fragile self-image as good. We hope that by placing others in the category of bad, we are somehow freed to inhabit the category of "good." Of course, we know this is untrue. Even a mildly honest self-assessment reveals that each of us has committed enough wrong to also safely inhabit the category of bad. In this context, the grace we offer ourselves becomes a type of false grace, an escape route fraught with deception. The irony is that as we journey with forgiveness and as grace emerges for the other, we discover that there may also be more grace available for ourselves. We are all both good and bad, both broken and whole. Herein is a hard lesson: those who resist grace for the other frequently lose the capacity to also regard themselves with grace.

During a workshop I was leading, the conversation turned to the topic of forgiveness. One participant stated somewhat strongly that we should not use the word *forgiveness* at all, as it is too burdened with religious overtones. Before I could respond, another participant jumped in: "I am not religious either," she said, "but forgiveness is far too important and far too special to be available only to religious people." She then went on to explain how significant forgiveness had been in her own life. The practice of forgiveness is sacred ground. When it arrives within our spirits, it is like a still, small voice that whispers hope into our broken hearts. "You too can be free," it says. "Free of what?" you might ask. The spirit replies, again in its still, small voice: "Hatred, pain, resentment, the need to be right, shame, guilt, burden . . ." As it speaks, the spirit plants a small seed of grace in our beings, so small we hardly notice it. But the seed grows, and as it does, we notice that grace has taken root in our souls. The new shoot of grace is so tender and vulnerable we find ourselves wanting to protect it, to keep it safe from being trampled by the vicissitudes of life. Still, it remains something of a mystery to us. Over time, grace grows. And as it does, the grace growing within us welcomes *us* home to ourselves. There is grace for us and our brokenness.

Slowly, an awareness settles on us: Grace is abundant beyond measure. The grace that welcomes us home is simultaneously welcoming the other. Embraced by this gift of grace, we find ourselves making space in our spirits for the person who did us harm.

Several years ago, I led a healing circle for a group that had experienced a difficult conflict. Over the course of the conflict, the group's leader had been treated quite badly by his colleagues in a fashion quite disproportionate to that of which he was accused. At the start of the closing round of the healing circle, I asked the participants what they wished to let go of and what they wished to embrace in order to move forward well with one another. When it was the leader's turn to speak, he was quiet for a few moments. Then he looked up and, speaking slowly, offered the following: *"I release my right to defend myself."* Every breath in the room became tentative in the moments after his statement. Not only was the leader's wound visible, but all the other circle participants knew that they had contributed to that wound. In one short sentence, the participants were convicted of their guilt and also released of this conviction. With this statement, the energy in the room shifted. Then the leader continued: *"And I embrace and commit to caring for and working well with each one of you."* It was a sacred moment. When the session was over, nobody noticed when I slipped out of the room into the foggy night. The participants were too busy reconciling with one another on the sacred ground created by the spirit of forgiveness the leader had offered.

Despite our attempts to define forgiveness, it remains always and to the end something of a mystery. Nothing can undo the harm done. Yet in some strange way, the dawning of grace somehow still heals. How is this possible? It is said that *hanging on to resentment is like drinking poison but expecting the other person to die.* Forgiveness is choosing to stop drinking the poison. It is about choosing life over death. Forgiveness is about releasing our right to be angry—and our right to defend ourselves, because our story can never be fully known and understood by those who have not lived it. Forgiveness honors our mutually incomplete, broken, we-have-not-arrived-yet selves. Forgiveness means we can freely acknowledge that we are each good and we are each broken. The hierarchy of who is better and who is worse is upended. A deep humility replaces hate, denial, annoyance, superiority, and any other form of resentment that has taken hold of one's being. No one finishes this race unscathed; yet all are beloved.

Barriers to forgiveness

Several months ago, a teacher shared with me a principle she follows when working with students struggling with behavior: "If they can, they will." If children can do better, they will. If they do not, it is because of whatever may be going on in their lives or in their bodies or within the learning environment.

Applying this same principle to a more general context, the teacher noted: "If people can be different during times of conflict, they will be different. I know this sounds strange, but to resolve conflict we need to lower our expectations of what people can do or could have done rather than focusing on what we expect from them."

While lowering our expectations of one another does sound odd, it is an important skill on the journey toward conflict healing. Perhaps without knowing it, this teacher had stumbled onto one of the key barriers to forgiveness: holding others to unenforceable rules—rules that dictate what we think others should or should not have done in their lives or in their conflicts with us.[3] Most people are doing what they can with the skills and resources they have and within the reality of the larger context of their lives. We cannot enforce rules of behavior on those for whom matching our expectations is simply impossible. "If they can, they will. If they can't, they won't." The teacher continued: "Whenever I go into conflict resolution meetings to *teach* the other person, things go poorly. If I go in to learn, things go well." The teacher is right. When we go in to learn and connect rather than to teach, we go in as equals. We meet at the level of the other's heart. When this happens, people feel heard. Ironically, although it can feel as if going in to learn means giving up the right to teach, it is when *we* begin with a learning stance that learning for the other also begins. In other words, when we go in to teach, learning does not occur. When we go in to connect, learning happens, almost as a byproduct of our connection.

Early in my career, a woman who wanted to resolve a conflict with her father came to speak to me. I listened, anticipating she would ask for mediation. Instead, after outlining her needs, she shared that mediating with her father would be difficult as her father had died some years earlier. We shifted then to a coaching relationship where we talked about what she would want to mediate with her dad were he still alive. She noted all the ways she wished her dad had been a different type of father. At some point, I asked about her father's life. She acknowledged that it had been difficult. He had been disregarded by his own father, had experienced considerable trauma, and had been forced by life circumstances to pursue a career far outside his skill area. At some point, she turned to me and said, "I suppose it is possible my father was doing the best he could, given who he was." While my client's sentiment does not negate the fact that her father was often unkind and absent, her insight released her from being enslaved by a standard for her father that he would never reach. I asked my client, "What if you let go of the rules you have for your father? What if you acknowledge that, for whatever reason, your dad *could not* obey the rules of what a really good father would have been? What happens then?" As my client responded, I sensed a burden being removed from her shoulders. She no longer had to carry bitterness about her father's inadequacy, or jealousy when she saw other fathers who appeared more than adequate. Instead, she could begin to accept her father as he had been.

There is a great mystery associated with what my client experienced that day: *When we can accept the complex reality of others, we can begin to accept ourselves and our own complexity.* If we are honest with ourselves, we are forced to acknowledge that none of us lives up to the standards of unenforceable rules. Over time, our inability to accept the brokenness of the people around us will turn on its head to become an inability to accept ourselves.

Holding on to unenforceable rules is only one of five barriers to forgiveness. A second barrier to forgiveness is our misguided belief that ruminating can change the past. This barrier is also known as the "if only" landscape. "If only I had not said that . . ."; "If only I had walked away from that conversation . . ."; "If only she weren't that type of person." Unfortunately, we cannot heal what we deny, and "if only" thought patterns are a form of denial. While learning from the past is critical and learning often involves imagining how we could have done things differently, "if only" can tantalize us with escaping into a fantasy of an alternative and impossible reality. "If only" also keeps us locked in a past, usually accompanied by our defended self. It is our defended self, after all, that plays into our "if only" thinking. This same thinking can cause us to project our defended past onto a hoped-for future, still governed by our attachments. Forgiveness, by definition, lives in the present by releasing us from the past and by freeing us to live into a new future.

How then do we learn from the past without getting caught in unhelpful "if only" thinking? In my work I often ask clients to describe their conflict experience and then to identify where things went awry. We consider these moments through the lens of diverse conflict principles and tools, imagining what each could have done differently. Sometimes I ask my clients to role-play their way through an old incident, this time shifting the story by making more life-giving choices in the critical moments of their conflicts. Not only does this retelling help ease the memory of the past, but it focuses on transforming the future through the principle that what we can imagine we can more easily do.

The difference between learning from the past and being caught in "if only" thinking is based on the form of personhood we bring to our explorations of the past. If our reflections of the past are like being stuck in a spin cycle, replaying that we are right and the other is wrong—or that we messed up and must self-flagellate to be redeemed—we are caught in a false-self system that only serves to entrench our conflict. If, instead, we bring our heart space with us as we wade into our conflict story, we view our past through the lens of our deeper self, opening space for a compassion-infused learning that simultaneously releases us from the past while returning us to the present moment—and to a fuller, more accepting embrace of our humanity and the humanity of the other.

The three remaining barriers to forgiveness are all closely connected to the intent-action-effect communication model we explored in chapter 1: seeing the other's intention as being about us, blaming the other for the impact something has had on us, and living from a grievance story. The fact that these dynamics function as barriers to forgiveness and also appear in a communication model drives home the point that our communication patterns and our capacity to forgive are deeply connected. It is a humbling thought: how we lean into our conversations with one another—even in times of relative peace—is correlated with our capacities for forgiveness.

Beyond their association with the intent-action-effect communication model, these latter three barriers to forgiveness share another commonality: All tend to place the self in the role of victim and the other in the role of offender. While genuine victimization can and does happen—the intention here is not to minimize this—in conflict it is common for the self to present as innocent while identifying the other as guilty, regardless of what actually occurred. To complicate matters, third-party players sometimes enter this dynamic, presenting themselves as the victims' rescuers. Rescuers and victims alike blame those they identify as villains for the harm that has occurred. Problems arise, however, when one seeks to find the person who will self-identify as the villain. Virtually no one will claim this title. Every victim is another person's villain, and every villain is a victim—or a rescuer. In the end, all claim innocence. We ignore our complicity; we blame the other rather than practice curiosity; we assume we can know the other's intentions; and when an experience is difficult, we tend to package it according to a grievance story—a narrative that casts us in the light of innocence.

Our latter three barriers to forgiveness create a curious problem for us: Why should identifying as a victim limit our capacity for forgiveness? Is this not what forgiveness is about—forgiving those who have harmed us? Indeed—for-giveness is about exactly this: forgiveness is about letting go of the power that an act of harm has had over us. And herein lies our answer to the victim-forgiveness conundrum. To let go of the power that an act of harm has had over us is to also let go of our victim identity. Similarly, if we are a third-party player, to let go of the power that an act of harm has had over another is to also let go of our rescuer identity. It is here that the reality of the grievance story becomes so important: When we have built our identity around a victim/rescuer narrative, letting this identity go in favor of forgiveness and healing can appear akin to letting go of our soul. Our grievance stories are attachments that function like an addiction. Releasing them involves going into a type of withdrawal. If we are no longer a victim, then who are we?

Into this dynamic, we are invited to recall that we are not our defended self, we are not our wounds, and we are not our grievance stories. We are not our shame and we are not our blame-driven thoughts, either. We are beloved.

And, in many of our conflicts, we are also complicit in one fashion or another.

The problem with blaming the other, seeing the other's intentions as being about us, and living by grievance stories is that we miss the diverse and complex ways we are also complicit. Perhaps we were too tired to speak well, perhaps we were defensive, perhaps we harmed another inadvertently. We may have operated out of underlying harmful biases. We may have reacted because, somehow, we felt that our selfhood was at risk. Perhaps our childhood trauma spoke through our attempt to address a current situation. Perhaps we were simply misguided. Perhaps we harbored hatred in our heart. What-ever the case may be, when we hold tightly to our identity as victim and place the other in the role of offender, our vision becomes myopic, limiting our ability to think creatively about how to respond to the conflict and cementing an us-them view of the world. More importantly, we miss seeing how we too can be a change agent in our own story. When we blame the other for the pain we have experienced, our healing is tied to the other's transformation. When we own the pain we have experienced as *our* pain, when we release our allegiance to our grievance story, and when we let go of our belief that we can know the other's intention, we become empowered to focus on our own healing. We learn to let go of the power the event of harm has had over us. As this occurs, we begin the pathway of forgiveness—first for ourselves and eventually also for those with whom we have been in conflict.

FALLING DOWN AND GETTING UP AGAIN

An old story echoes often in my mind: A woman living near a monastery wonders what the monks who inhabit the monastery do all day. One day, she encounters a monk outside the monastery walls and asks: What do you do in there all day? The monk smiles and replies: We fall down and we get up again.

I have always enjoyed this story. It speaks to me of humility and the frailty of the human condition. It also speaks of the great courage required to repair whatever our falling down has broken. The story assumes that each one of us falls down. Falling down, it appears, is a normal part of the human condition. Each of us gets it wrong sometimes. Each of us fails, sometimes in big ways. If this is true, if falling down happens, how do we get up again?

Imagine for a moment a literal fall to the ground. Getting up again involves multiple steps: (1) reorienting our body so that our head, torso, and limbs can work together again; (2) straightening our body; and often (3) tending to our wounds before stepping forward once more. These three stages of recovering from a fall—reorienting, straightening, and tending—function as metaphors for us, representing our own journeys through those conflicts where we have fallen down.

Reorientation

Conflict is disorienting—including when we are aware that our actions have harmed another person, whether or not this was our intention. Becoming aware of the harm we have done forces us to consider a question most of us would like to ignore: *Who am I that I have done this thing?* The temptation is to dispense with this question by denying that we have done harm. Alternately, we may blame the other or the context for the harm we have caused. Indeed, there may be truth to our blame: the context and the actions of the other often do play a role in what occurred. Ignoring or denying our complicity, however, keeps us rooted in our defended self, limiting our ability to heal our relationship with the other. By definition, building our home in our defended self also limits our own healing and our own capacity for joy. If blame and denial are two temptations in response to our complicity, then a third temptation is shame. Considering our complicity is hard work. It takes us to uncomfortable places and disorients us.

Denial, blame, and shame limit our capacity to reorient ourselves to the possibility of taking responsibility for the harm we have caused: Some believe, for example, that to apologize (or even to consider one's culpability) means to see oneself as lesser than, or as no longer better than. Others fear that to take responsibility for one's own actions is to acquiesce, to let the other person off the hook. Some have come to regard the other as lesser than to the degree that the other is not deemed worthy of an apology. Still others offer that the person who was harmed is too sensitive—it was not their intention to do harm, they say, and as a result no apology is necessary. Unfortunately, each of these assumes a hard separation between self and other, assumes that the well-being of the people in our lives is not our responsibility. Each also reveals the close association between our complicity and our sense of selfhood: If questions are raised about our intentions and our actions, we may fall into our defended self and its corollary shame. So we avoid our complicity, falling into our defended self regardless. Reorientation challenges us to engage an inner journey, reminding us that we can take responsibility for our actions without losing our selfhood.

Straightening

When we straighten after a fall, we are able to look around and to see clearly once more. In conflict, after our reorientation and coming to terms with our complicity, we are invited to cast our gaze to the other, to confess the harm we have caused. While the word *confession* is most often used in a religious context, like *forgiveness*, this word is too important to seal away for religious use alone. Confession is the physical act of taking responsibility for the harm we have done. Confession invites a spirit of humility—a spirit that is able to commit to the journey of building better relationships even while recognizing our failures along the way.

Confession goes by many names: taking responsibility, apologizing, atonement, accountability. Under whatever name it comes, the act of confession is profoundly freeing. Perhaps this is because an inability to apologize is associated with a decreased sense of personhood. Being unable to apologize for harm we have created declares that our identity lies with our defended self. In contrast, an apology unhooks us from our defended self, making a return to our heart possible. Said most simply, an apology allows us to move on.

A good apology involves several key steps:

1. To begin, we may offer a general apology. We may know we have messed up; an apology reveals our positive intent and levels the playing field between self and other.

2. As a second step, we are encouraged to listen to the other's story, to hear the other's pain and the impact that our action has had. During this phase it can be critical to ask questions to fully understand the pain we have caused.

3. As a third step, we offer a second specific apology, alongside an expression of regret. Having heard the details of the pain we have caused, we are able to be specific about the actions for which we are apologizing—and for the impact our actions have had on the other person. A specific apology has an impact that a general apology can never have. By offering details about the harm we have done based on what we have heard, we communicate that we have heard and understood the pain we have caused.

4. Our fourth step offers what we will change to ensure a transformed future. The following quote, attributed to Archbishop Desmond Tutu, makes the point: "If you take my pen and say you are sorry but do not give me my pen back, you have not apologized." We cannot promise that we will not fall down again—indeed, we will fall down again. What we can offer is our best efforts to engage our relationship differently in the future. In some cases, this may include tangible acts of restoration, some version of returning the pen that we have taken.

5. Finally, there are times when in our apology conversation it is appropriate to ask whether the other would value

an explanation of our intent—without explaining our harm away. While we do not want to make excuses for our actions, information about our intent—given without defensiveness—can help heal a broken relationship.

Put together, our apology may sound as follows: *I know my actions harmed you; I'm sorry. // Can you say more? What impact did my actions have on you? // . . . When I made those remarks, they had a significant impact on you. I'm sorry. I regret the pain my actions have caused you. // In the future, I commit to not making this type of remark. // Are you open to hearing what was going on for me when I made those remarks? What was going on for me that day does not excuse my actions, but it might help you understand the larger context of that day . . .*

To give an apology is a vulnerable act. On one level, an apology carries risk—after all, our apology may not be accepted. But there is more: Offering an apology is like an unveiling, revealing to self and other our defended and false self. It is as though we are exposed. An apology declares our frailty to all who are listening and confesses that we too have fallen down. There is a mystery here. So often our defended self holds us in its grip, yet in some strange way, an apology has the capacity to dissolve this grip. While our apology may not be accepted by the other, it nonetheless restores us to ourselves, loosening our allegiance to our defended self.

Tending

Even after an apology, how does one get up after a night of wrestling with feelings of "I can't believe I did that"? In the absence of self-compassion, our self-awareness of the harm we have done and the apologies that follow can take on a punishing spirit. Indeed, a life practice of confession for harms we have done is not really possible without self-compassion. Sadly, over time, self-awareness and confession alone can feel like a commitment to staying on the ground after our fall, to remain broken and entrenched in our pain. The corrective is to tend to our wounded spirits, holding ourselves with a spirit of grace.

Grace invites us to regard ourselves and the other with compassion, even as we commit to the ongoing work of navigating the difficulties in our relationship. Grace honors the reality that on this life journey, we will fall down. Grace partners with confession and self-awareness to empower us to get up again, and to continue the work of building better relationships with one another. If self-awareness and confession alone keep us on the ground after we've fallen down, it is grace and compassion that allow us to find our feet and walk again.

CONFLICT CONVERSATIONS

One of the skill sets we are encouraged to employ when seeking to transform conflict is to nurture the capacity for both-and thinking—seeing the truth in both self and other. Even in cases of deep divisions, we can work to understand one another's truths, though we may disagree with the other's conclusions. In a recent *On Being* podcast,[4] Anglican bishop Michael Curry reminds us of the value of listening deeply, beyond the finer points of each other's arguments, in order to hear the life stories that form us and our opinions. "Tell me the story of your life that brought you to the conclusion that you happen to hold," Curry offers. Mediator Joe Schaeffer echoes this same impulse when he asks parties to discuss hard topics over which they disagree—but to begin each sentence with "I remember when . . ."[5]

Both-and thinking invites us to share truth from our perspective while listening for truth in the other's perspective; it says we can hold boundaries and forgive at the same time; we can be committed to our principles and to compromise. We can see the good and the brokenness in self and other. Both-and thinking honors that self and other are both two and one.

To get to the place of both-and thinking, we must move beyond our minds, beyond our technical conversations, to meet one another at the place of our hearts. Recently, I was speaking with a client, Zosha, about her experience after a mediation session. The meeting had gone well enough—both sides told their stories and made concessions regarding what each could have done differently. By the end of the session, the two parties seemed to understand each other at the head level. At the heart level, however, a chasm remained.

During my conversation with Zosha, she said to me, "Since the last session, I have spent considerable time thinking this through and clarifying my position on the matter." I listened. Then I offered: "It is good you have clarified your position. I wonder . . . what would happen if you also clarified your heart?" During our conflict conversations, it is possible to reach an agreement only at the head level, finding a way to move forward on various technical matters. Our peace with one another is vulnerable to being lost, however, when our heart and head are not aligned. The heart is always interested in something more, something greater than what the head will demand and concede. Indeed, when we are only in our head, we tend to become locked in place. Rigidity takes over our mind and body, making us unbending and making our spirit hard to access. Naturally, this makes the resolution of conflict difficult. And while conflict conversations in this context are possible, and sometimes even necessary, achieving satisfying outcomes is difficult. Without a bit of softness, trying to solve conflict between two hard-minded parties is like biting into a green peach. It is unpleasant.

When appropriate to do so, engaging well in conflict conversations is possible—either directly or with third-party support. To talk well with one another, we are wise to follow several key steps:

1. Self-reflection. Take time to think about what occurred and to imagine what the other person's intentions may have been that have nothing to do with you; reflect on your intentions, how you were affected, your backstories, your grievance story, and your complicity. Notice where your ego was hooked, where you became attached, and how you fell into your defended self; accept your descriptive self without judgment and make your way home to your deeper self. Re-centered in your deeper self, intentionally discern whether it is appropriate to talk directly with one another, and if yes, set up the conversation.

2. Set up the conversation. Invite the other for a conversation and choose a safe and neutral space to speak with one another.

3. Plan for the conversation. What would you like to say when you are together? How do you want to "be" in your spirit? If you are so inclined, pray and meditate to re-center yourself in your deeper self. Practice self-compassion and compassion for the other. Ready your spirit for the encounter you will be having.

The conversation

4. Delight. Once you are together, take time to delight in one another, to connect and to remember your mutual humanity. This is such an important step, yet so easily overlooked.

Conversations are always strengthened when we begin on a foundation of mutual care. Moreover, it is difficult—even impossible—to engage in truth telling outside of a container of trust. How we begin determines the energy we bring to and carry through a conversation.

The imagination of this step also acts as a test: if you cannot entertain the possibility of regarding the other through the lens of delight, it is likely best not to meet with one another without support.

Once you have delighted in one another, set the focus for your conversation: What have you come to address?

5. *Discover.* Listen to one another and learn from one another. Share your understanding of the conflict that occurred between you. Tell your stories of what occurred. Give space to hear each side fully before digging into each point of view. As you speak, remember to honor each other's personhood, take responsibility for what is yours, and practice curiosity, being open to what the other may need you to hear. Determine what the "problem as problem" is while avoiding making the other person the problem.

6. *Deepen.* Deepen your understanding of the situation by asking open-ended questions and paraphrasing to ensure understanding. Risk sharing why the conflict affected you the way it did. Risk hearing why the conflict affected the other party the way it did. Use the intent-action-effect model and the building blocks of communication, discussed in chapter 1, as guardrails to support your conversation. Listen for the moments in the conversation where grace can break through. Make space to honor these moments when they occur.

Many people like to jump from "discover" to the next step, "discern," while ignoring the "deepening" phase. Deepening the conversation, however, is critical for true transformation to take place. This is where you see each other's heart and learn about the life stories that have brought each of you to the conclusion or conclusions you hold.

7. *Discern.* Discern and develop a next-steps plan. What will you need to do to repair that which has been ruptured? What commitments can you make to ensure continued understanding and goodwill moving forward? A next-steps plan can be as simple as an expression of goodwill, or as detailed as concrete action steps that will change the nature of the relationship going forward.

Take time to summarize the outcomes of your meeting—where you have agreed, where you may still have differences, the insights you have gained, and the commitments you have made. It is tempting to end the meeting without summarizing the outcomes. Unfortunately, when this is missed, you may exit the meeting with different memories of what occurred. Reviewing and summarizing the meeting means both parties are more likely to leave with a common understanding of what occurred.

After the conversation

8. *Getting back in stride.* After a conflict conversation—even a good one—it can be difficult to get back into stride with one another again. The rupture may be repaired, but in many cases the relationship may not feel normal yet. Reaching out after conflict conversations is a courageous act. This is especially challenging when the conflict conversation was not entirely satisfying. It involves learning how to walk with one another all over again. It involves a dogged commitment to moving beyond your pain to seeing the humanity of the other. And in some cases, it may mean parting ways.

CONFLICT TRANSFORMATION: A SUMMARY

Conflict will occur. The invitation to each one of us is to lean into these hard moments, risking the possibility of transformation. Often, though not always, leaning in involves risking meaningful and hard conversations with the person or persons with whom we have had conflict. While multiple practical tips and tools can help us navigate those conversations well, "salting from the inside" reminds us to also lean into our deeper heart center. Rooted here, we find ourselves able to draw from a well of grace—for ourselves and, over time, also for the other. Grace allows us to be present to ourselves and to our lived experience of pain and struggle; it invites us to recognize our complicity and, when we are ready to do so, to forgive those who have caused us harm. While we do fall down, grace allows each one of us to get up again. And in some miraculous way, grace sometimes even allows us to reach a hand toward the other, helping the other, too, get up again.

Chapter 5

Conflict Transformation and the Practice of Spiritual Disciplines

When conflict happens, it has a way of uprooting us and spinning us out of control. At these times, it is easy to fall into our defended self. We become defensive, sometimes unknowingly, only to realize later that our response to the other was driven as much by our defended self as it was by what the other had done. We may feel we are right to the degree that we become angry and spiteful. We may feel misunderstood and may wonder how the other could think so negatively of us, when in our minds our intentions were positive—or at least legitimate. We may feel wounded and hurt, even debilitated by the conflict in our lives. In our worst moments, we may forget that we are still beloved, regardless of what has occurred. Recently, a friend of mine shared with me how after a season of tending to hard conflicts, her nights had become unbearable because of the negative self-talk that consumed her thoughts. My friend is not alone. We who long to be people of grace and healing must also walk hard journeys of self-reflection. At times, this self-reflection can become too much, turning from a healthful self-awareness to a form of self-harm. When this occurs, or when we feel so deeply wounded or defensive that we hardly recognize ourselves any longer, how do we ground ourselves again? How do we return to our deeper self? This chapter explores several spiritual disciplines to guide us along this journey.

Each of the disciplines in this chapter can be placed somewhere on a continuum of spoken prayer at one end and silent meditation on the other. Depending on their nature, mantras and guided meditations lie somewhere between the two ends of this continuum. While these forms of prayer and meditation differ from one another in a variety of ways, each shares the intention of returning us to our center, to the heart of God, where we find our selfhood—and where we also find the selfhood of the other.

THE DISCIPLINE OF PRAYER

A friend of mine worked as a hospital chaplain early in his career. One day a woman called for a visit from the hospital chaplain. She had gone into labor well before her due date and wanted him to pray to God to end her contractions. My friend stumbled a bit with his words. He told her somewhat sheepishly that one cannot really control God, and who knows what prayers can do? The woman retorted, "Aren't you a minister? Do you not believe what you preach?" She was strong and insistent. My friend began praying, now somewhat urgently. As he prayed, the woman began to repeat some of his words, almost as if pulling them into herself. When my friend ran out of words, the woman insisted that he continue, telling him that one does not need words in order to pray. My friend continued praying, now speaking aloud only occasionally. Eventually the woman fell asleep and my friend returned home. The next day he learned that the woman's contractions had indeed stopped and she had been discharged from the hospital.

Whether or not we are people of faith, many of us call for help from a higher power when we are in crisis or when we are deep in conflict. In this regard, we are not that different from my friend. We call to a higher power, but also stumble with trust. Do we really believe that this higher power can act in the problems in our lives? James Finley, himself a survivor of great suffering, states, "God's love can save you from nothing, but it can sustain you through anything."[1] I affirm Finley's statement. But I also know that I have experienced the presence of a great mystery, and that I have been at the crossroads of improbable coincidences, including acts of mercy. How do we regard this mystery? This larger conundrum is beyond the scope of this book. What I can affirm is that the presence of a love-that-is-greater-than-us sometimes bowls us over, surprises us, and pulls us, as though with a tether, out of our suffering and back to our heart and to a sense of oneness with God.

Praying to be saved from our pain

Over the course of my career, I have been called on several times to coach people through their post-conflict recovery. In some cases, the conflict was not extreme and the person coming for coaching simply wanted to learn from what happened. But in other cases, what began as conflict at some point tipped over into extreme harm. And in still other cases, the relationship between the parties danced between normalcy, conflict, and great harm, leaving my clients both wounded and confused. Those who had been on the receiving end of extreme harm described their experience as "crazy making." Over time they began to doubt themselves; they made blunders they would not normally make; and they experienced a type of life-and-death vulnerability they had not known before. In extreme cases, these clients described fearing for their lives—even after the aggressor had moved on.

It was after hearing a client's experience of being on the receiving end of great harm that I understood in a new way what it means to pray to be saved. Before this experience, I had never really warmed to the Christian language of "sin and salvation." From what and for what are we meant to be saved? And then this conversation appeared in my life. For my client, this experience—not of sin but of suffering—was soul crushing. Certainly, if one looked hard enough one could have found that my client had not been perfect in her actions. Nonetheless, none of my client's missteps warranted the degree of harm to which she was subjected. Her experience was so intense she feared for both her life and her livelihood. My client described how, in her worst moments, when even the act of breathing was difficult, she called out to God to save her from her aggressor.

My client is not alone in her pleas for help. In our worst moments of pain, we long to be reknitted to a larger, grace-filled universe, to know we are not alone, and yes, to be saved. We cry out in hopes that someone or Someone is listening, that our lives can be spared, and that we too may be whole again.

My client shared with me that after she cried out in her pain, she began to notice small miracles and wonders in her life: A card from a long-ago friend, an article that came across her desk that spoke to her situation, a family member who called to check in. My client began noticing that in one dream after another, the hand of God appeared on her shoulder, saying, "Watch me. I've got this. It's going to be okay."

It is said that near-death experiences can be clarifying. The near-death experiences of extreme conflict can also be clarifying. While it is not an experience anyone would wish for, extreme pain can put us into a liminal space. We stand on the threshold between life and death, knowing that if we are given life once more, we will come back as different people. We will have been changed. But how? Do we come back bitter and volatile? Or do we come back more whole, more open to goodness, generosity, and grace?

In his book *Immortal Diamond*, Richard Rohr states that there are three things in life of which we can be assured: The first is that we are beloved. Regardless of what we have done in our lives or what has been done to us, this truth remains: We are beloved. We are worthy. Second, suffering will come. Life does what life does. In one fashion or another suffering will be thrust on us. This includes the suffering of conflict. And finally, when we are in our time of suffering, a hand will reach toward us to pull us back into life.[2] That hand may come in the form of a friend, a kind gesture from a stranger at the grocery store, a therapist, or an article that crosses one's desk. This hand may also come in our dreams— whether waking or sleeping—when we sense the hand of God on our shoulder telling us, "Watch me. I've got this. It's going to be okay."

Another kernel of wisdom is embedded in this collection of "three things of which we can be assured." While most of us do not desire conflict or seek it out, some degree of suffering appears to be critical to our transformation. When we live only at the first stage, the stage of our belovedness, we can become complacent, falling into attachments, even unknowingly. Suffering has a way of rocking our boats, waking us up, and calling us forth into transformation and back into life and to the love that calls us into being. This includes the suffering of conflict. None would desire the suffering of conflict; nor would anyone call the suffering of conflict good. Nonetheless, it appears that in our times of great suffering we somehow see the presence of the divine more clearly. The wisdom here is that the way up is sometimes the way down, that a letting go, a release, a surrender of our attachments is critical for our development.

In those times when we cry out to be saved, we discover that we need saving not only from the aggressor. We also long to be saved from our fears, our self-doubt, our desire to run away. Herein is a strange mystery that we will see again and again in our lives. When we receive our fears as our own, we release ourselves from our aggressor's grip. Said otherwise, when we own our feelings, we are empowered to differentiate from our aggressor. Our fears, after all, are also a form of attachment, of keeping us bound both to our defended self and to the aggressor. While our fears initially protect us, over time they can imprison us. When we recognize our fears as ours, as part of us, we are encouraged to show care to our fearful self. When this occurs, our fear can find its rightful purpose in our beings, as a clarion call that awakens us, driving us back to our hearts. Now, standing on a solid foundation where selfhood is never at risk, we can discern what a healthful response to the other may be.

Recently, I was speaking with a European colleague who said of a client with whom he was working, "I know the people want to get this conflict over with as quickly as possible. But I think they need to go through it to really allow it to do its work. This conflict is necessary because if they allow it, it will transform them."[3] It is conflict, after all, that can finally help us let go of old and unhelpful patterns that no longer serve us. My colleague was not saying that people must stay in abusive situations. Rather, he was saying that conflict can sometimes be our teacher, demanding self-reflection, discernment, learning, and action from us. The verb, *demanding*, is important here. Conflict is a hard teacher. What if in the chaos of conflict we are asked to pause, and to actually use this moment of difference to discover what it means to be human? My colleague compared the rush to a resolution to a desire to reach the resurrection without first spending time in the death pangs of the cross. Moving through conflict is not easy, especially if the conflict has been painful, has triggered old wounds and narratives, or has continued for a long time. Yet . . . we find grace, including for ourselves, when we engage in the hard and difficult work associated with our transformation. Sometimes, it is in engaging our brokenness that we become whole. In a strange way, sometimes our conflicts save us.

Praying for angels

Sometimes our prayer is less about being saved and more about being sustained. It is about needing to sense a hand of grace near us as we engage in hard conflict conversations.

Several years ago, I found myself in a conflict with a dear friend regarding a situation that was complex and fraught. We both wanted what was best for each other; neither of us fell into hatred for the other; and while each of us talked about this situation with mutual friends, and while talking about rather than with one another created an additional layer of misunderstanding, the intention on both sides was never to do harm. The intention was simply to share the load of our pain. We were mutually broken by a very complex situation. The situation was difficult enough that we could not easily navigate our way back to each other.

I knew that someday we would need to talk with one another about what had happened. I also knew I needed to wait until the time was right. But when would this time be? For eighteen months, the timing just didn't feel right. Then, one night, I had a dream that we were talking together around a campfire. For me, this was a sign. The time was now. But how to begin after eighteen months? In an email to my friend, I asked for her forgiveness even as I offered her my forgiveness. She offered that we could meet to talk; I agreed, and we set a date for a few weeks hence.

I was nervous about meeting my friend and so, for some reason, I prayed for angels to somehow be present during our conversation. At the time, it was not my spirituality or my inclination to pray for angels, but it is what I did.

Our meeting was to take place at a coffee shop on a Saturday evening, early in the new year. On that Saturday afternoon, my family and I were at the local hardware store looking for a new toboggan. As we stood among the toboggans, I realized we would need a cart. I left my husband and children in the toy section and returned to the front of the store for a cart. The store was almost empty. As I sailed through the aisles with my cart, my eye was drawn to a couple who appeared completely out of place. While we were in rough work clothes, this couple was dressed in long white coats. While we looked unkempt, they shone. I was sure they couldn't be local. When I saw my husband, I said, "There is a couple in the store, and they shine. They look out of place, like angels from a movie."

Saturday evening, I left the house to meet my friend. I was anxious. I wanted the conversation to go well and didn't want to add to the pain between us. When I got to the coffee shop, my friend was already there. I took my seat, facing the window.

About fifteen minutes into our conversation, the couple from the hardware store walked by on the sidewalk outside the café, still in their long, flowing white coats! I had forgotten about this couple and about my prayers for angels. Now this couple was walking by the window of the café. I was surprised. I had been praying for angels, and here was this couple that I had described as angels only a few hours earlier. A little smile crossed my face, and I returned my focus to my friend. My friend and I talked. We used every skill set we knew to ensure we had a good conversation. And the conversation went well. We clarified misunderstandings, apologized for our parts in the conflict, and agreed that the situation had become bigger than both of us. It was a good meeting. Near the end of our conversation, I accidently dropped a coin on the floor and bent down to pick it up. As I did, I saw for the first time the people at the table sitting slightly behind me. It was this same angelic couple, alongside another couple. Delightful surprise came over me, followed by a feeling of grace flowing over and through me like a waterfall. The angels hadn't just walked past us on the sidewalk, they had come in and sat at the table closest to us in the coffee shop. And there were not two but four people at that table: If the hardware store angels were my angels, was the second couple a set of angels sent to care for my friend? Had angels come for both of us? I was awestruck.

Were these two couples truly angels? My head says no but my heart says, "Maybe?" They could have been random strangers who happen to shine and who enjoy wearing white coats! What I do know is that my prayer, together with the presence of this couple, caused me to trust deep in my bones that my tough conversation with my friend was not happening in isolation. It was happening in the presence of a greater grace that was cheering us on, grounding us, and inviting us into mutual participation in this greater grace.

Praying for healing from our complicity

As we have seen, coming through conflict well involves a journey inward, a recognition of the pain we have experienced, and a hard look at our own complicity in the conflicts in which we have participated—or the conflicts we have seemingly avoided. This is not as easy as it seems, since most of our complicity in conflict is associated with some form of our attachment. Some contribute to conflict out of frustration because of the dynamic that has arisen between themselves and another person. Some people believe they have no conflict yet leave unease and pain in their wake. Some avoid meaningful conversations because they fear the risks naturally associated with close relationships. Some actively create conflict where none is necessary or where a softer approach may be more effective. Some use conflicts in the here and now to fight the ghosts of their past or to fight the unresolved issues in their lives. Some harbor hatred in their hearts while outwardly acting as though all is okay. Still others blunder their way into conflict quite unknowingly. The list could go on.

Praying for healing from our complicity involves walking through a valley of pain. Most of us do not want to be found on the side of what was done wrong. Yet there is profound freedom in the ability to say, "I did this. This was not my best self. I am sorry. I was wrong." Taking responsibility for our guilt or complicity shifts us out of a victim stance. The more we claim our contribution to conflict, the more we become a change agent in our own story. From this stance, it becomes easier to "cleanly" hold the other accountable. Rather than being driven by our defensiveness, our conversations with the other about the other's complicity are now about finding a path forward rather than about convincing the other and us that we are right. We are freed to take a learning rather than a teaching stance with the other. Healing a broken relationship becomes possible.

Taking responsibility for our portion of conflict involves contending with our guilt. We do not relish feelings of guilt, nor do we wish to be torpedoed into the shame that so often flows from feelings of guilt. The distinction between guilt and shame is critical here: guilt is easier to recover from; shame, in contrast, tends to drive us further into blame and conflict. Guilt says I did a bad thing; shame says I am a bad person.[4] Shame dissociates us from our deeper self, from the place within where perfect goodness resides. Shame declares that our descriptive self is flawed. Defined by our defended self, shame says we must protect ourselves to stay alive. It is why shame is so often converted into blame. And when that is not possible, shame turns inward, causing us to die inside. Guilt says, "My selfhood is not at risk *and* I did a bad thing for which I can take responsibility." Guilt can even say, "I have lived by a life pattern that has contributed to great suffering, for which I take responsibility—and my selfhood is not at risk. My heart still has a home in the heart of the divine that loves me unconditionally."

When we pray for healing from our complicity in conflict, we offer our complicated, broken, complicit selves to the love that first called us into being. We learn to forgive ourselves. And we fall, often exhausted, into arms of grace that declare to us the first truth of which we can be assured: We are beloved. We are still beloved regardless of what we have contributed to the conflicts in our lives. In this embrace, we now find the courage to sort our attachments, and to practice the skill of letting go of at least a few of the attachments that caused us to fall into unhealthy conflict in the first place.

Praying for those suffering our pain

One of the reasons conflict can be so debilitating is that it can feel as though nothing is in our control. It can seem like we are at the mercy of the other person's healing journey. In response, it is worth contemplating what we can control. One such area of control is the observation that our pain is not ours alone. Many people around the world share our pain. They too have found themselves in painful conflict, wishing that they had acted differently. They too have felt wounded by the actions of others. It is possible to link the pains of the world together with ours, drawing our breath not only through our pain but also through the pain of those whose stories are like our own. In this case, we pray words of acceptance for our pain ("I accept my feelings of pain"), followed by words of acceptance for the world's pain ("I take into my soul the pain of those in the world who are experiencing what I too have experienced"). When these two steps are complete, we can add two more steps to our prayer: release of our pain and release of the world's pain ("I release to God and to the universe my feelings of pain; I release also the world's pain").

When our own pain is acute, we may not yet be ready to receive the pain of the world. In a sense, opening ourselves to the pain of the world functions like a measuring stick. When we are able to carry in our spirits not only our pain but the pain of the world, we know we have taken a step on the road to healing.

Praying for the person (or persons) with whom we are in conflict

When we are in conflict, we may long for a quick and easy resolution. There are circumstances, however, that demand we give each other space. In these situations, we can do more than

wait. We can pray for the other, we can spend time in meditation, and we can engage in self-reflection to understand our
part in the conflict story. All of these things are like plowing
the field of our souls, readying us for the time when a conversation about our conflict becomes possible.

In some of our conflicts, praying for the person with whom
we are in conflict is quite natural. This is true whether we have
been wounded or have contributed to wounding others, and
whether the conflict is large or small. In other conflicts, we
can pray for the other but doing so is hard work. And in some
cases, praying for the other is a responsibility we allow others
to carry for us.

What does it mean to pray for the other? It can be as simple
as wishing the other well. It can be as profound as praying
for God's light to shine on the other person. It can include
expressions of love and hope for the other's well-being. It can
also include our wish for the resolution of the conflict.

I am inclined to use the following prayer: *God, embrace
this person with your arms of loving-kindness.* While we may
be unable to embrace those with whom we are in conflict, it is
possible to pray that an energy of love that is greater than us
do so on our behalf. As we pray this prayer, we will find that
our own hearts also soften. We cannot simultaneously entertain vengeful thoughts and prayers of loving-kindness for very
long. Soon, the prayer changes *us*. Even if the other person
has done us great harm, the loving-kindness prayer honors
the other's personhood even in the midst of our pain. In cases
of extreme pain, we may find we cannot even pray for God to
love this person. In these situations, we allow others to take up
the task of praying for the one who has harmed us.

Praying for the other is correlated with the spiritual
discipline of seeing the other in the fullness of the other's

humanity—including the person's deeper, descriptive, and defended selves. This is not the same as giving someone a free pass. Instead, it is a dogged commitment to see the humanity of the other, to recognize both the brokenness of the other and the other's potential for goodness. It is about regarding the other with compassion, even as we hope compassion is extended to us for our complicity in whatever has gone awry. It is about remaining committed to seeing the face of God in the other. Sometimes this commitment is associated with the spoken prayers we offer. Sometimes it is a wordless commitment.

THE DISCIPLINE OF MEDITATION

When we experience situations of conflict, several physiological processes converge to protect us—but which take us away from our deeper self. Our heart races, our stomach turns, our breath becomes shallow, our brain shuts down. Perhaps our legs wobble. We may react too quickly; we may become locked in place; or we may flee the situation altogether. With the passage of time, our body comes to rest—though, if the event was traumatic or if it belonged to a larger pattern of similar events in our lives, our body is not so much at rest as it is primed, lying in wait until the next occasion for self-defense emerges. Similarly, while some conflicts allow our mind to come to rest, others continue unabated in our self-talk, as we engage in defensive and sometimes obsessive thought patterns. In short, we become stuck.

One of the most important disciplines associated with forging a path back to our deeper self—and to the presence of the divine—is the practice of meditation (not to be confused with mediation). Meditation is rooted in a diversity of religious traditions and goes by many names, including centering prayer, mindfulness meditation, and simply, meditation. Defined most simply, meditation is the act of engaging in intentional or guided silence. The practice of meditative silence is broadly known today as a therapeutic practice—it helps still the body and the mind, promising great health outcomes. While there is truth in this—and while the therapeutic gift of meditation should not be minimized—there is more to meditation than a stilled body and mind. The practice of meditation returns us to our heart, to our deeper self, to the presence of God coursing as breath in and through our body.

Meditation for compassion and healthy boundaries

While we may pray for the other and hold the other with compassion, it is important to recall that compassion for the other is strengthened by the maintenance of healthy boundaries. This is a paradox: we offer compassion—an energy that brings us nearer to the other; and we hold boundaries—an energy that puts distance between us and the other. Living with this paradox involves engaging both energies at the same time. After all, if we are only boundaried, we lose the other; if we are only compassionate, we lose ourselves. It is also true that if we are only boundaried, over time we also lose ourselves—the self cannot survive without connection. Similarly, if we are only compassionate, we lose the other—the other cannot survive with too much connection. From the perspective of spiritual disciplines, how do we offer both compassion and boundaries at the same time?

For the past number of years, I have taught workshop participants to consider two hand gestures to reflect the balance of compassion and appropriate boundaries. While our left hand is held like an open cup in a gesture of welcome and grace; our right hand is held up and out like a stop sign to gesture our boundaries. Recently, I became acquainted with a guided meditation[5] that leans on these same hand gestures for those times when we are navigating tricky relationships with others. I offer a modified version of this meditation here:

1. Sit comfortably, with feet to the ground and with a strong back.
2. Take time to breathe and to settle into your body.
3. Hold your left hand open like a cup. Receive the spirit of the other in your open hand with grace and compassion.
4. After several minutes, raise your right hand in front of you, like a stop sign. Set and maintain a boundary between yourself and the other, in a spirit of strength (but without judgment).
5. After several minutes, cross your arms over your chest. Hold yourself with self-compassion.
6. Repeat steps three to five until your meditation is complete.

So often, we are tempted to resolve our conflicts by obliterating our boundaries, opening ourselves to more pain, or we take the alternative approach, maintaining iron-clad boundaries that are meant to protect us but instead only imprison us. Meditating with an open hand and a boundary-setting hand teaches us how to live in the paradox—allowing us to honor our need for safety even as we regard the other with a spirit of grace.

Silent meditation

The human spirit appears to be hardwired with longing—longing for the world to make sense, for meaning, for a sense of safety in another's arms, for a sense of belonging and unity with the greater spirit that also longs for us. James Finley writes:

> The core of our being is drawn like a stone to the quiet depths of each moment where God waits for us with eternal longing. But to those depths the false self will not let us travel. Like stones skipped across the surface of the water we are kept skimming along the peripheral, one-dimensional fringes of life. To sink is to vanish. To sink into the unknown depths of God's call to union with [God] is to lose all that the false self knows and cherishes.[6]

To meditate is to sink into the embrace of God who longs for us. But, as Finley suggests, while we may long for this embrace, we also resist losing ourselves in the unknown depths of union with God. Our false, defended self simply cannot let go. It is because of this that we meditate: to *practice* letting ourselves sink and vanish into this embrace. Meditation silences mind and body; it releases us from our restlessness and from the compulsion to endlessly think, whether that thinking is about grocery lists, flights of glory, conflicts, obsessive thoughts, or any other false-self distractions. To be clear, the goal of silent meditation is not to *achieve* perfect silence. The goal is to *practice* silence. A focus on *achieving* silence simply turns meditation into another project whereby we can judge ourselves as either a success or a failure, creating an attachment and thrusting us back into our defended false self.

Meditation is the practice of sitting still, becoming conscious of our breath, and releasing thoughts and distractions as they arise. It is the act of returning to silence—returning to our center, the divine presence within. Some forms of meditation encourage the person meditating to slowly repeat a short phrase or mantra until thoughts fall away and a type of inner silence is found. Another stream, known as centering prayer, invites the person meditating to enter silence immediately, and to use a "sacred word" to return to silence whenever the mind wanders. Some use the same word or mantra for years; others modify their word or mantra for the season in which they find themselves.

Stilling the wandering mind and returning to our center is not easy to do. This is why most meditation traditions include some word or mantra to assist with stilling the mind. As thoughts enter our mind, we are encouraged to recognize our thoughts and, using our word or mantra as a gentle guide, return to silence. Our mantra is like a walking stick, helping create a rhythm in our being, stilling the fretful nature of our anxious mind. Along the way, we are also encouraged to attend to our breath; we breathe in slowly; we breathe out slowly. Every breath in and every breath out is a return to our center, our deeper self, the presence of God alive within us. Experienced meditators may stay in this silent space for twenty minutes or more, twice per day. When I teach the discipline of meditation, I tell people to start small—perhaps one minute or two, five or fifteen—and to work their way up from there. I propose the following rhythm to get started:

1. Find a comfortable space to sit, either cross-legged or in a chair. Sit with a strong back (it is easier to stay awake this way). If you wish, use a few moments for spoken prayer.
   a. Notice your body, its aches and pains. Settle your body. Soften your face.
   b. Observe the thoughts you have brought with you. Release them and settle your mind.
   c. Attend to your feelings; acknowledge them and release them too.
2. Set a timer for your meditation.
3. Begin. Notice your breath. Breathe in and out.

4. Matching your mantra to the pace of your breath,
    repeat your mantra. If you fall into complete silence,
    be there. If your mind wanders, notice that it has
    wandered and return to your mantra, your center. If
    your mind settles on a story of pain, release this story
    and return to your mantra. If your mind tantalizes
    you with delightful and elevated thoughts, release
    these and return to your mantra. (Remember that
    these delightful thoughts will still be waiting for you
    after you leave your time of meditation.)
5. End your meditation. If you wish, offer a prayer to
    close your time of meditation.

Meditation is not easy, because the mind wanders *a lot*. But
this is sort of the point. The discipline of stilling the wandering
mind lies at the heart of why meditation is so important in
life—and for situations of conflict. I think of meditation as
going to the gym for our soul. When we go to an exercise
gym, we build our muscles in order to be strong in the 24/7
of our lives. When we spend time in meditation, we build our
centering muscle, allowing us to return to our center in the
24/7 of our lives. Each time we still our wandering mind, we
reknit ourselves to the foundation of our being. A wandering
mind simply means a more intense workout, and in the end,
stronger centering muscles. With time, we will find ourselves
strengthened not only in our meditation but also outside our
meditation. It will become easier to return to our center when
obsessive thoughts, conflicts, and worries seek to crowd our
mental space.

The practice of meditation does not change us overnight.
In fact, many have told me that their interpersonal relationships became worse rather than better in the first weeks and

sometimes even months of their meditation practice. In other words, they had more rather than fewer conflicts after they began meditating. Why? I suspect that when we begin to meditate our old patterns become more accessible to us, and not always in the most delightful ways. The good news is that as our patterns are brought into the light of our awareness, we can actively contend with them. We may discover behavior and thought patterns we thought we had released. Our transformation takes time. Meditation teaches the discipline of accepting and releasing our thoughts and our patterns, allowing us to slowly but surely release our way of being that has caused us to fall easily into our defended and false self, our allegiance to how things have been between us and others, our way of regarding ourselves and others.

One of the challenges associated with meditation is learning how to regard the wandering mind with grace rather than judgment. Many walk hard journeys of self-judgment related to the wandering mind, sometimes giving up on meditation altogether because stilling the mind is so difficult to do. But the wandering mind is not the problem. The challenge lies in regarding our wandering mind without judgment. Finley offers the following words of solace to those struggling with the wandering mind: "In meditation we are all beginners. Some of us are just more seasoned beginners than others."[7] Another contemplative, Thomas Keating, offers the following story on the same theme. After twenty minutes of silence, a nun protested: "I'm such a failure at this prayer. In twenty minutes I've had ten thousand thoughts!" Keating responded, "How lovely—ten thousand opportunities to return to God."[8] Meditation, it seems, provides an excellent opportunity to practice releasing our false-self inclination toward judgment over and over again. Every release from judgment exercises the muscle of self-compassion, a muscle which also leads naturally to compassion.

Meditation is no panacea. We will fall down and we will need to practice getting up again. Nonetheless, meditation gives us a taste of freedom. It makes a discipline of returning to the heart of God, to our deeper self. As we increasingly find ourselves in this home, we experience more wonder, more joy, and more wholeness even amid hardship. Centered in our heart, it becomes easier not to fall into unnecessary conflict, and to return to our center when conflict does arise, allowing us to be more discerning in our response.

MANTRAS FOR THE 24/7 OF LIFE

One of the most surprising kernels of wisdom that I have learned, mostly the hard way, is this: *What we resist we entrench.* Of course, this statement needs further explanation: I am not suggesting that we are meant to welcome slavery, injustice, or abuse. In my experience, however, our ability to respond thoughtfully to slavery, injustice, and abuse is limited by our denial that these realities are, in fact, happening. The Black Lives Matter movement knows this in its bones. It is white denial, after all, that has aided and abetted systemic racism for many years.

There are many realities that we resist. We resist taking an honest and hard look at ourselves, limiting our ability to see the harm we impose on others. We resist acknowledging the life patterns by which we live that provide us with readily accessible albeit life-limiting explanations about why our lives are as they are, or why we believe we are lesser than or greater than those around us. We resist our painful feelings, either distracting ourselves from them or obsessing over them—both of which are a form of resistance. What we resist we entrench.

And what we entrench tends to cause us to fall into conflict with others.

Allow-accept-release-rest

Several years ago, I was invited to mediate a dispute between two sisters whose relationship had gone awry. Given the depth of pain on both sides of this dispute, the mediation went as well as could be expected. In the end, the two women agreed to remain friendly with one another, though they would no longer seek time together outside of family gatherings. They did not want to damage the larger family unit, but with so much pain under the bridge that spanned the space between them, increasing their time together was too much to ask.

Some years later, one of the sisters came to me for a coaching session. She was distressed with the ongoing division between her and her sister. During our session she shared with me that she thought about this broken relationship with her sister multiple times per day. The broken relationship had become like an addiction, consuming this woman's thoughts and feelings for several years. At some point in the conversation, I asked my client if she could give me six weeks of his thinking time. She was puzzled. I proposed that for the next six weeks she live by the following mantra: "I accept that this relationship is broken; and I release this broken relationship into God's care." If this woman wanted a longer version of this mantra, she could repeat the following: "I allow myself to feel the brokenness of this relationship; I accept that this relationship is broken; I release this broken relationship into God's care; and I rest in God's love for me." (For those who prefer, I recommend an alternate version of the latter portion of this mantra: "I release this broken relationship, and I rest in self-compassion.")

This mantra is based on several key principles:[9]

Allow. We must *allow* ourselves to feel our pain. As we let the pain of our experience enter our bodies and as we notice the places in our bodies where the pain becomes lodged, we acknowledge that the pain exists. We allow ourselves to feel it. And we allow it to be ours. In a sense, we digest our pain, making it easier to be released.

A few months ago, I received disappointing news that an award I was told to anticipate had not materialized. When the phone call came, I immediately felt a surge of sadness course through my body. My mind went to negative self-talk ("I didn't deserve this award anyway"). I sensed a type of disappointment-energy seeping into my body. I was afraid that this disappointment-energy might influence my upcoming conversations, so remembering the principle of *allow*, I headed out for a walk. As I walked, I repeated to myself: *Allow yourself to feel your disappointment. Allow yourself to feel your pain.* I took time to notice where in my body my pain was lodging itself. By the time I had returned to my desk, the pain was digested. I shared my disappointment with a few people later in the day, and as I did I noticed that my disappointment was not laced with either pain or negative self-talk. It was just a point of fact. And it was gone. Naturally, some pains are much larger than a missed award and some pains will take significantly more time to digest; yet if we allow ourselves to feel our pain, we cut short its ability to drive us in circles, to distraction, or to cause us to do harm.

When I first began experimenting with this mantra, I only used the *accept* and *release* portions. After I became somewhat adept at the two-stage version of this mantra, however, I realized that my brain was good at saying "I accept" when in fact it was really saying, "Yes, I accept already—let's move on to release." When this happened, release was like a street fight that usually ended in a draw. In other words, we can't fake our way to release. As a result, I needed to add the *allow* stage of this mantra to create space for myself to genuinely sit (or walk) with whatever I was experiencing. When that happened, the rest followed much more naturally.

Accept. The second step of the mantra is the step of acceptance. Before we can release our pain, we must accept it. Perhaps acceptance is similar to the step of allowance, but in their energy, allow and accept are different from one another. To allow myself to feel my pain is to notice where in my body, mind, and spirit the pain is making itself felt. To accept my pain is to recognize that this pain is uniquely mine. Owning our pain as our own is the first step to stopping its transference. It is also a critical step in our discernment regarding how to respond to our pain. In a sense, accepting my pain as mine is an empowering act. It is *my* pain. If I can own the pain as my own, I can begin to do something with it. If the pain is not my own—that is, if I seek to reject it—I will fall into one of several traps, such as denial, "if only" thinking, avoidance, distraction, blame, or displacing the pain onto innocent passersby.

Release. After we have allowed and accepted our pain, we release it. For some people, it is helpful to release their pain to God or to the virgin Mary; others prefer releasing it to the universe; still others into the molten lava at the center of the earth. The idea here is that the pain we are carrying is not ours to carry alone. The universe—or God's care—is large enough to receive our pain, to tend to our wounds, and to restore us to life. When we release our pain, we release the power the pain has over us. We let it—whatever it is—go.

The stage of release includes a word of caution. I have often encountered people who say something like, "I have just let go." Or, "We all just need to let go and move on." There is wisdom in these words; someone is holding fast to something that is keeping this person bound. Often, however, we try to convince ourselves and those around us that we have let go when we have not. When someone scratches the surface of our false letting go, that which is held in pours out. The pain was never far from the surface. In these cases, "let go" was more likely "held tight," placing the one who has engaged in a false letting-go at risk, should a retriggering event occur, of being catapulted back into pain and conflict. The mantra we have been exploring is instructive for us: release (or the act of letting go) is not the first stage of our mantra, it is the third.

While the experience of release is powerful, it is also true that for the big pains in our lives, we will likely need to return to the mantra many times. It is not uncommon for the metaphorical pain pathways in our bodies to be so well trodden that we readily and repeatedly fall into these pathways even against our better judgment. How do we stop the often unhelpful ways of thinking that we have developed to help us manage our pain? When the ruts of our minds are deep, we need a steady hand on our thought patterns in order to keep our minds from falling into these ruts once more. This is why mantras are so helpful—they function as this steady hand. It takes time and commitment to develop new ways of relating to our pain. Some mantras are with us for three weeks, sometimes six, sometimes even more—always without ceasing when we are in a season of great pain.

Rest. The final stage of our mantra is rest—in God, in self-compassion, or both. Why self-compassion? One of the biggest barriers to our healing is our inability to love ourselves. The truth is, we all mess up sometimes. We all feel pain. And most of us tend to get down on ourselves. Without self-compassion it is difficult to heal. Without self-compassion, it is also difficult to be compassionate to others. When we meet people who are very judgmental, it is likely that they have spent a significant portion of their life journey being judgmental of themselves. In the vast majority of the conflicts we experience, each person connected to the conflict has played a part in the conflict's unfolding. A hard and honest look at ourselves is critical for learning and healing from conflict. But a hard and honest look at ourselves is also painful. Self-compassion allows us to say, "I messed up, and I am still worthy." For those who nurture a relationship with God, resting in God's love provides deep comfort and reminds us that we are beloved.

When I began experimenting with this mantra, I used the "accept and release" form of the mantra everywhere: in difficult conversations, at the grocery store, in traffic. It became a nonstop mantra or breath prayer for me. I also noticed as I journeyed with this mantra that there is much to accept and release. "I accept that I am frustrated with the conversation I just had. I release myself and the other person into God's care." "I accept my frustration with this traffic jam. I release my frustration with this traffic jam." "I accept that I am frustrated with my tendency to become frustrated. I release my frustration with my unfinished self into God's care. I rest my unfinished self in self-compassion." Finley describes our false-self attachments as a never-ending series of scaffolds.[10] With every scaffold we remove, another presents itself for removal. Sometimes discovering our scaffolds is painful. Over time, it can also become a grace-filled experience as we welcome the diversity of scaffolds that make themselves known to us, awaiting release.

Several years ago, I was working with a woman who was frustrated with her colleagues and wanted a mantra to better navigate her workplace context. As we talked, I asked her what mantra she was already using. She was confused. She said she was looking for a mantra but didn't already have one. I then asked her what words went through her mind on her way home from work. "Oh," she said, "that's easy. Every day, I tell myself, 'You idiot. Why did you do that?' Or, 'Why did you say that stupid thing?' It happens every day." I replied that clearly she already had a mantra—just not a very good one. Her mantra, "I am an idiot," was contributing to her malaise at work and to her inability to effectively manage the conflict in her workplace. I asked her then for a more helpful mantra. She offered that she could say, "I need to try harder." We discussed this for a while. I pointed out that she was already trying hard and that the mantra to try harder could easily be construed as a whip with which she could lash herself at the end of each day. In conversation we came up with another mantra: "I accept that what I gave to my workplace today was my best. I release all that is undone and rest in self-compassion."

The allow-accept-release-rest mantra functions as a base mantra upon which additional mantras can be built. Conflict-healthy mantras involve the following principles:

1. They accept self and other exactly as they are.
2. They accept the pain of the current moment without ducking this pain.
3. They speak a healthy truth into being.

In my work, I have helped people custom-design mantras for their unique situations. Some mantras have been given to me by healthcare providers who have accompanied me at critical junctures of my life. Many follow the allow-accept-release-rest rhythm. Some borrow the principles of the allow-accept-release-rest mantra but do not follow the rhythm so closely. A sampling of these mantras is as follows:

- "I accept the other person exactly as this person is—without any hope of this person changing. I accept myself exactly as I am—without any hope of myself changing." (Note: The second phrases, "without any hope of me or the other person changing," are critical, otherwise we can deceive ourselves: we accept the other person with the hope that our acceptance will change that person—and it better be fast! Interestingly, it appears that it is only when we accept others exactly as they are that change becomes possible. Acceptance comes first.)
- "I am beautiful, I am worthy, I am beloved."
- "We are both worthy."
- "I am afraid and hold myself and my fear with tenderness."
- "May God embrace this person with arms of loving-kindness."
- "This is my body; with it I am well pleased."
- "I release to God and to the universe all the pain and sorrow from every cell in my body."

A mantra for our micro-judgments

The more we become attuned to the deeper self and the delightfully neutral nature of the descriptive self, the more we will be confronted by the micro-judgments we make of others, whether these occur while we are in meetings, walking down the street, or dealing with those with whom we disagree. Micro-judgments are so common that they play in our minds like background music we hardly even notice. They may seem banal and benign—so long as our micro-judgments are only in our minds, do they matter? They do matter. Our micro-judgments contribute to the undying nature of our underlying biases—biases which have a concrete impact on how we relate to those around us, whom we hire, with whom we choose to speak at social events, and so on. Our micro-judgments also persist in keeping us locked in the defended self. After all, judgments such as these tend to sort our society according to a metric of who is better than and who is lesser than. When our micro-judgments are about those with whom we have been in conflict, these judgments limit our ability to see the full humanity of the other. They also constrain our return to the deeper self, the birthplace of goodness, generosity, and grace. In situations of conflict (or as a life pattern), our micro-judgments can function like a gateway. Once we walk through this portal, we open our spirits to even more judgment, and to falling into the us-them trap.

How do we manage the micro-judgments that arise within us? To begin, it is worth celebrating when we actually *notice* our micro-judgments, given how endemic they are. Noticing is a first step. Challenges emerge with what to do next: the temptation is to self-flagellate, to judge ourselves for our judgment. Unfortunately, this strategy tends to backfire, making us only more judgmental. Instead, a more helpful strategy is to offer compassion to ourselves and to the other when we have fallen into the micro-judgment trap.

Several years ago, I began using the following mantra, borrowed from Indigenous Hawaiian healers, whenever I noticed an internal micro-judgment regarding another person: *I love you. I'm sorry. Please forgive me. Thank you.*[11] I say this mantra (in my mind) to the person about whom this judgment was made. I also say this mantra to myself—apologizing to myself for the micro-judgment I just made. Naturally, the other person knows neither about the micro-judgment nor about my mantra in response. This conversation is happening within me alone. Nonetheless, something quite remarkable happened after I began using this mantra: my micro-judgments decreased. The mantra takes a moment of judgment and transforms it into a brief but meaningful healing moment—for ourselves and for the space between ourselves and the other person. We always transition more easily from judgment into grace when we embrace ourselves and others with a spirit of compassion.

Mantras when the pain is unbearable

In the last pages of her book *When Things Fall Apart: Heart Advice for Hard Times*, Pema Chödrön quotes Jean-Paul Sartre as follows: "There are two ways to go to the gas chamber: free and not free."[12] In a similar vein, Viktor Frankl, himself a survivor of Nazi concentration camps, writes in his book *Man's Search for Meaning*, "When we are no longer able to change a situation, we are challenged to change ourselves."[13] Likewise, in his book *The Courage to Create*, Rollo May writes, "Human freedom involves our capacity to pause between the stimulus and response and, in that pause, to choose."[14]

What do we do with the optimism reflected in the quotes provided by these three men—especially when two of them are speaking about an injustice as horrific as the Holocaust? Is human freedom from the "sins of the other" possible? Can we actually change ourselves to the degree that we can be free even in the face of terror? And if we could be, what would actually be different about how we experience the world? In my work I am sometimes exposed to great trauma, including in those who have been on the receiving end of conflicts that have tipped into significant harm and abuse. When the abuser still wields power, what options do the traumatized have?[15]

Part of becoming "free" involves holding a clear boundary between what is ours to hold and what belongs to the other to hold. This is like saying in one's mind and with unconditional positive regard to the person creating harm, "Your journey is yours to walk and not mine. I will not become a host to the pain you seek to give me. I return your journey to you and invite you to care for that which is yours." In situations of pain, it is strangely tempting to hold not only that which is ours to carry but also that which is the other's to carry. We are burdened not only by our own pain but also by our fear of the other and our expectations of the other. While we can practice unconditional positive regard, holding the other's story by virtue of pain or expectations ties our healing to the other. We are now shackled to the other's ability to heal, left waiting for when the other will be transformed before our healing can begin or be completed. Setting a grace-filled line between ourselves and the other frees both of us to walk our own journeys at our own pace.

Of course, our capacity for self-deception makes this commitment tricky: it is not easy to discern between what is ours to carry and what is not ours to carry. It is logical perhaps to focus on our contribution to harm. But there is something else we must carry that is harder to determine and even harder to grasp. This is our internal emotional process that hooks us unhelpfully to the other's journey. A boundary encircles each person, a protection of one's selfhood. In situations of extreme conflict, the walls of this boundary can be broken. We can become bowled over by another's volatility, and be hooked in ways we did not think possible. A meditative spirit, also described in chapter 1 as the practice of presence, involves observing—without judgment—the feelings that arise within us and, ironically, embracing these feelings. It is the denial of what arises within us that keeps us hooked. Becoming free involves becoming friends with the feelings that we are experiencing, because these are *our* feelings. They do not belong to the other. They belong to us.

The first step of the mantra involves recognizing the feeling emerging in us. Is it fear? Is it anger? Hurt? Betrayal? Where does this emotion sit in one's body? What is its shape? What does it do in us and to us? *I allow myself to notice the <fear> arising within me. I notice its impact on my body. I see how it is causing me to spin out of control.*

The second step involves recognizing that this emotion is a part of us. This may seem common sense, but so often we give the other power over our emotion. We believe that our emotion is somehow the other's, and that we need the other to change for our emotion to change. It is an empowering act to say, "This is my emotion. I accept it as mine." *<Fear>, I accept that you are a part of me. I know you are my <fear> and I welcome you as a part of me.*

The third step involves being kind to our emotional state, to hold ourselves with tenderness. Years ago, I read a book by Thich Nhat Hanh in which he wondered why we are so harsh with our wounded selves. If our child is wounded, he said, we would not disregard or berate the child. Instead, we would collect the child in our arms, embrace it, and speak tenderly to it: "It will be okay. You will be okay." We can do the same with ourselves. *I comfort you, my <fearful> self. I hold you, my <fearful> self, tenderly in my arms. I love you.*

A fourth step returns us to our mantra, *I release myself into God's care and rest in self-compassion.*

When we own our feelings as our own, when we do not take on that which is not ours to take on, and when we regard the other with compassion, we maintain a healthy boundary that encircles us. Our selfhood is now not at risk, allowing us to become discerning once more about how to respond to the situation around us.

WE DO NOT HEAL ALONE

Several years ago, I was working with a client who had been through an exceptionally complex situation. By the time she left her workplace, she had been traumatized and needed to attend to her healing. She described to me how she had repeated mantras, more or less without ceasing. She prayed for healing, for the burden of her pain to be lifted. She accepted and released her feelings. Despite her best efforts, she could not center herself. Finally, she was able to speak with a therapist and to me, her coach. She told both of us that she needed us to center her because she could not do it for herself.

Together, my client and I were reminded of an important lesson: We are not meant to heal alone. During this experience, several friends, colleagues, and therapists surrounded my client with love and care. They held her upright when her legs could only wobble. They centered her when her capacity to center herself had reached its limits. They helped her reconnect to her strength. They helped her heal. We cannot carry our pains alone—nor are we meant to. We heal in the care of one another.

As noted in chapter 2, one of the accusations sometimes leveled at the world of mindfulness and contemplative spirituality is that while we may be at peace, the world around us is very much not at peace. Most teachers of contemplative spirituality and mindfulness argue that this is a misunderstanding of the discipline. Mindfulness is only mindfulness when it includes a focus on the other and on the health of those around us. In short, mindfulness is not intended as an individualistic act. I have always agreed with this idea. But on this journey of healing with my client, I saw the dangers of individualistic mindfulness in a new way. Individualistic mindfulness states that I am responsible for my own healing; I can be the master of my own groundedness. While there is naturally much to be said for taking responsibility for our healing, I have become aware that there is also a gift in recognizing our limits. We are not meant to be on this centering journey alone. Yes, we meditate, we pray, we practice our mantras, and yes, these center us. And . . . along the journey of life, there are times when we lean on others to center us for us. It is not because we are weak. It is because we are not meant to walk our hard journeys alone. A hand does reach toward us to return us to life.

Recently, I received a text from a friend who was about to walk into a hard conversation. She wrote that she couldn't find center and she knew she needed to in order to be strong for the conversation she was about to have. As I was about to walk into a tricky conversation myself, I wrote the following to my friend: "I'll center you and you can center me. We'll do it for each other."

A "LETTING GO" EXERCISE

All good therapy, mindfulness, preaching, meditation, contemplative prayer, mantras . . . seek to return us to our deeper selves, to root ourselves in the heart of God in order to reestablish our relationship with our descriptive selves and one another. There is, however, one additional discipline that I recommend, but only to those who are able. It is the discipline of intentionally letting go of our attachments.

When I was in my mid-twenties, I decided to engage in a thought experiment. As far as I know, the idea for the thought experiment simply came to me, unbidden. I did not know then that this experiment was a time-tested but not so commonly known spiritual discipline. I found it profoundly meaningful and have returned to this discipline in various ways throughout my life. The discipline is as follows:

1. Make a list of all your characteristics, strengths, limitations, ego needs, attachments, aversions, relationships, roles, and responsibilities . . . (As you can see, this can become a very long list!)
2. One by one, recall to your mind each item on your list. Actively visualize yourself letting each item go, one by one. Depending on your inclination, you may visualize yourself simply releasing this item, giving it over to God, or allowing it to flow through your feet into the molten center of the earth. Some you will find are released quickly. Others will require more time to release.
3. Pay attention to what emerges as and after you release each of your attachments.

When I engaged in my early homemade version of this exercise, I released one characteristic after another until there was nothing left. Absolutely nothing. Without any characteristics to hold my sense of selfhood up, I arrived at a point of nothingness. I found myself staring into an abyss. It felt somewhat frightening. But I also knew I was teetering on the edge of something sacred. And then the sacred became visible. It was just as Thomas Merton had described it, though I only came to know of Merton's work later: the place of perfect nothingness is the beginning of everythingness. I touched holiness, and knew in that moment that the truest form of selfhood involves a type of unity with God—a unity which I could see only after each descriptor was released.

Sadly, we cannot stay in those moments forever. Life does what life does. Buddhist teacher Jack Kornfield delightfully titled one of his books *After the Ecstasy, the Laundry*.[16] And not just laundry. Life. Work. Tough decisions. Conflict. Our less-than-best selves. The journey of our transformation happens in fits and spurts, sometimes with grandeur but more often in the tough slog of thinking things through, making choices, falling down, and getting up again.

Several years ago, one of my clients did this same exercise. He described feeling trepidation as he came to the point of nothingness. When I asked him how it felt to experience nothingness, he described a freedom he had not felt before. He was worried though. Did releasing his characteristics mean he could no longer enjoy being a brother or a friend? I proposed that the journey of letting go allows quite the opposite to become possible. When we hold our characteristics tightly (as an ego attachment), it is like holding our characteristics in a tight fist. No air or light is allowed in and our beloved characteristics begin to suffer. If, however, we hold our characteristics with an open hand, we appreciate them without attachment, allowing both life and joy to become possible.

Several times over the past number of years, friends have shared with me about the journey of death taken by loved ones in their lives. In some cases, especially when the person who died is young, they describe how their loved ones shed their characteristics one by one. They released their sense of themselves as someone who "produces." They released their independence as others cared for them. They released their identity as parent, sibling, child, spouse. It was a radical letting go of their attachments to their descriptors, of the burden of navigating their descriptors and, to some degree, of the descriptors themselves. Often, letting go results first in pain and then in something more akin to exhilaration and freedom.

The good news is that we do not need to wait until our deathbed to experience this exhilaration. We can die before we die. Jesus describes this as losing your (ego-attached) life so that you can find your (centered) life again. In other words, when we are able to let our characteristics go, they return to us, now unfettered from our attachments, allowing ourselves to stretch more fully and more wholly into the cloak we were given to wear at our birth.

Conclusion

In 1993, I had the privilege of mediating for the first time. In my very first case, I was primarily the observer, watching as my co-mediator navigated the conversation between the parties. It was a victim-offender case, sent to us by the courts in hopes that a resolution to the conflict could be hammered out in mediation rather than in a courtroom. The conflict involved two men, Dan and Al, who in principle were friends. In reality, however, Dan, together with a circle of friends, regularly bullied Al. On a particularly horrific occasion, Dan and his friends were able to ply Al with enough alcohol that Al became very drunk. The men placed Al in several compromising positions, and took photos of Al in this state. In the days that followed, the men showed these photos to Al, mocking him and shouting slurs at him. Al was horrified and ashamed. In deep pain, he lashed out at Dan and his friends, destroying some of Dan's property. Quickly hiding the photos, the men called the police. Al was too ashamed to tell his side of the story. In the end, Al was charged with damage to Dan's property.

Al maintained his silence about his experience of the event until we were well into the mediation, telling neither the police nor us, his mediators, what happened. During the mediation session, it became clear that something was off. Dan was cavalier, ready to quickly "let everything go." Al, in contrast was visibly uncomfortable. My co-mediator and I called for a break, then met individually with Al, followed by Dan. In our conversation with Al, the larger narrative of what had taken place finally emerged. Al wept. Normally, in mediation we would invite Al to tell his side of the story in the mediation room. In this case, Al was not ready, nor did he feel safe doing so. With Al's permission, we sent the case back to the courts, this time with a note detailing the larger narrative of what had occurred from each party's perspective. While one could argue that the mediation "failed"—it did not contribute to a resolution between the parties—the mediation succeeded insofar as Al was finally able to share his side of the story with someone who cared enough to listen.

The story involving Al and Dan is tragic, laced as it is with abuse. One could also argue that the two men began their interactions with one another well into their defended selves, although in very different ways. Already before the encounter between these two men, Al felt profound shame about his social skills and status. He was lonely and vulnerable to being targeted by Dan and his friends. Dan presented with such bravado and disregard for Al that we could only assume he was covering a deep shame that he wanted no one to see, least of all his friends.

What would be required for Dan and Al to come home to themselves again? I did not have the opportunity to engage in this question with the two men, but perhaps we can place ourselves in their shoes. It is tempting to align with Al and to repudiate Dan, to see ourselves among the good alongside Al, while rejecting those who are bad, including Dan. The advice of this book, however, takes us in another direction. We may not share Al's or Dan's life stories, but in our oneness, both

Dan's and Al's journeys are also reflected within us. Like Al and Dan, we too have made our home in our defended selves. Like Dan, we too have harmed others; we have divided the world into those who are "in" and those who are "out"; and we have shamed those who differ from us—sometimes directly and sometimes through the larger social systems in which we participate. On the other side of the conflict, we, too, have been on the receiving end of harm, to the degree that we also have lashed out in our pain. Like Al, we have sometimes hidden our pain, turning our pain inward until finally we cannot hold it in any longer. When this occurs, how do we come home to ourselves again?

There is a path, available to each of us. It is not an easy path to walk, involving as it does the removal of layer upon layer of our dragon scales. There is great pain in this removal because over time we have come to love the scales that imprison us. In the first instance the scales protected us; over time, the scales simply became comfortable to us. The path that we are asked to walk asks us to risk removing our scales. This path, which leads to our heart and the possibility of joy, is lined with hope. We are not meant to walk this path alone. If we open our eyes to it, we will see a hand reaching toward us, ready to be grasped as we are able to do so, ready to pull us forward, back into life, back to the place where we hear the voice of God calling to us, "You are my beloved, with you I am well pleased."

Now walls begin to tumble. We see the lie of our defended self; see the delightful neutrality of the descriptive-self cloak we were given to wear, and we see the other with eyes of compassion that earlier appeared unavailable to us. The space between us begins to clear of its fog. Now we can discern anew how to heal this space, making room for both self and other to breathe again.

Acknowledgments

I began writing this book not long after the start of the COVID-19 pandemic, and it appears it will be released just as we will be seeing the impact of mass immunizations. What a strange year it has been—full of hardships for so many, yet nonetheless marked with moments of wonder and grace. As I write this, immunizations are beginning to roll out. There is hope around the corner, hope that at the very least, we will be able to hug one another once more. Times such as these remind us just how valuable community is—even when we differ from one another. We need each other to be well. I also needed the support of many others to produce this book!

First—a big word of thanks to the people at Herald Press, including Amy Gingerich for inviting me to write this book, and Aimee Moiso and Sara Versluis for your fine editing eyes. You have helped this book become much better!

This book picks up several themes I first wrote about for my doctoral thesis. I owe a debt of thanks to Fernando Enns, my thesis supervisor, whose kindness and willingness to engage in wide-ranging conversations were and continue to be both inspiring and supportive. Many others also supported me through my thesis and the defense process, including my co-supervisor, John Paul Lederach, and the readers brought together by the Vrije Universiteit Amsterdam to review my thesis.

A big thank-you goes to two readers, Liz Walz and Karen Cornies, who read the text, and who along with Aimee Moiso gave feedback when the manuscript was still unrefined (this is a feat of great kindness). Liz, Karen; my sisters, Anita Pries and Monika Pries-Klassen; and my mother, Anganeta Pries, cheered me on so many times through the writing of the text. It is always so much easier to write with a cheerleading team on the sidelines.

Throughout and before the pandemic, my life has been enriched by regular walking partners who have made my life fuller and whose words of wisdom find their way into my thinking and in various ways into the pages of this book. Thank you! Thank you also to my friends and family—here in Canada and across the world. The wonder of technology has often brought you right into my writing space, allowing the space between us to be small even when we have had to be at a distance, whether because of geography or the pandemic. The gift of your kindness and care gives meaning and purpose to my life—and to this work.

So much of what I know is because of the incredible people who have invited me into their lives over the years, including clients, workshop participants, and students. Your questions, the challenges you have faced, your trust and goodwill, your willingness to share your stories with me, and your openness to allow me to test ideas with you—all of this has been an incredible gift to me. You have been my teachers, in more ways than you can ever know.

A deep bow of gratitude goes to my colleagues at Credence, both past and present, whose patience with my exploration of ideas, whose care, and whose incredible capacity to turn ideas into practice is awe-inspiring. I can't say enough about how grateful I am for you. Thanks also to my colleagues at Mediation Services under whose tutelage, many years ago, I got my start in this field.

My daughter, Anya, has so kindly taken an interest in my work. My sons, Thomas and Stefan—they mostly entertain me with their shenanigans. Thank you to each of you for making my life so much richer. And finally, my biggest word of thanks goes to my beloved husband, Paul Fieguth, whose calm and steady presence is my solid ground. Words can never express how grateful I am for you. *Thank you.*

Notes

INTRODUCTION
1 All names and identifying information have been changed in all the stories of conflict referenced in this book.

CHAPTER 1
1 While the definitions provided in this section are my own, credit belongs to both John Paul Lederach and Speed Lees, whose conflict escalation models I have worked with for many years. Their fingerprints are no doubt on what I have written.
2 For more, see the work of Roger Fisher, William Ury, and Bruce Patton in *Getting to Yes: Negotiating Agreement without Giving In*, 2nd ed. (Penguin Books, 1991).
3 Patrick Lencioni, *The Advantage: Why Organizational Health Trumps Everything Else in Business* (San Francisco: Jossey-Bass, 2012).
4 In conflict theory, this is called dispositional versus situational attribution. An action is blamed on someone's character rather than on extenuating circumstances. See K. Allred, "Anger and Retaliation in Conflict: The Role of Attribution," in *The Hand book of Conflict Resolution: Theory and Practice*, ed. Morton Deutsch and Peter T. Coleman (San Francisco: Jossey-Bass, 2000).
5 John Paul Lederach, *The Moral Imagination: The Art and Soul of Building Peace* (New York: Oxford University Press, 2005), 42.
6 Jonathan Haidt, *The Righteous Mind: Why Good People Are Divided by Politics and Religion* (Vintage Books, 2012).
7 For more information on this idea, see Eugenia Cheng, *The Art of Logic* (Basic Books, 2020).

8 Cheng.

9 Depending on the theorist, these can be described as more than five.

10 This model is modified from the work of Mediation Services in Winnipeg, Manitoba.

11 "Religion Doesn't Cause Religious Violence: A Conversation with Rabbi Sacks," interview by Mary Hynes, CBC Radio's *Tapestry*, April 6, 2016, modified August 6, 2020, 54:00, https://www.cbc.ca/radio/tapestry/religion-doesn-t-cause-religious-violence-a-conversation-with-rabbi-sacks-1.3511152/.

12 Marcel Proust, *Sodom and Gomorrah*, vol. 4 in *In Search of Lost Time*, quoted in Jack Kornfield, *After the Ecstasy, the Laundry: How the Heart Grows Wise on the Spiritual Path* (New York: Bantam Books, 2000), 187.

13 Brené Brown explores the idea of numbing and joy in her TED Talk "The Power of Vulnerability," filmed June 2010 in Houston, TX, TED video, 20:23, https://www.ted.com/talks/brene_brown_the_power_of_vulnerability.

14 For more on self-compassion, see Kristin Neff, *Self-Compassion: The Proven Power of Being Kind to Yourself* (New York: HarperCollins, 2011).

CHAPTER 2

1 Dorothee Sölle, *Silent Cry: Mysticism and Resistance* (Minneapolis: Fortress Press, 2001), 213.

2 As referenced by Beatrice Bruteau in "Prayer and Identity," with an introduction and commentary by Cynthia Bourgeault, chap. 4 in *Spirituality, Contemplation and Transformation: Writings on Centering Prayer*, Thomas Keating et al. (New York: Lantern Books, 2008), 85.

3 This section borrows from the work of Thomas Keating, and is described as "emotional programs for happiness." For more, see Cynthia Bourgeault, *Centering Prayer and Inner Awakening* (Lanham, MD: Cowley Publications, 2004), 136.

4 See Beatrice Bruteau, *Radical Optimism: Practical Spirituality in an Uncertain World* (Boulder, CO: Sentient Publications, 2002), 79.

5 Thomas Merton, *Conjectures of a Guilty Bystander* (New York: Image Books, 1989), 158.

6 James Finley, *Christian Meditation: Experiencing the Presence of God* (New York: HarperCollins, 2004), 6.

7 The idea of the difference between the image and likeness of
   God is described by Richard Rohr. See Richard Rohr, "In the
   Beginning and the End," Center for Action and Contemplation
   "Daily Meditations," December 31, 2017, https://cac.org/
   in-the-beginning-and-the-end-2017-12-31/.

8 As retold by Sölle, *Silent Cry*, 161–65.

9 Sölle.

10 Martin Buber, *Between Man and Man*, trans. Ronald Gregor-Smith
   (London: Routledge Classics, 2002), 22.

11 Buber, 23.

12 Buber, 22.

13 Betty Pries, "Bridging the Self-Other Divide: Conflict Transformation and Contemplative Spirituality in Dialogue" (PhD
   diss., Vrije Universiteit Amsterdam, 2019), 7, http://hdl.handle
   .net/1871/56123.

14 Lois Gold, "Mediation and the Culture of Healing," in *Bringing
   Peace in the Room: How the Personal Qualities of the Mediator
   Impact the Process of Conflict Resolution*, ed. Daniel Bowling and
   David Hoffman (San Francisco: Jossey-Bass, 2003), 183–201.

15 Thich Nhat Hanh, "Call Me by My True Names," in *Peace Is
   Every Step: The Path of Mindfulness in Everyday Life* (Bantam
   Books, 1991), 121–22.

16 To read Hanh's full poem, visit https://plumvillage.org/articles/
   please-call-me-by-my-true-names-song-poem/

CHAPTER 3

1 As retold by Jack Kornfield, *After the Ecstasy, the Laundry: How
   the Heart Grows Wise on the Spiritual Path* (New York: Bantam
   Books: 2000), 26–27.

2 For more on this idea, see Cynthia Bourgeault, *Mystical Hope:
   Trusting in the Mercy of God* (Lanham, MD: Cowley Publications: 2001).

3 James Finley, *Following the Mystics through the Narrow Gate:
   Seeing God in All Things* (Albuquerque: Conference at the Center
   for Action and Contemplation, 2010).

4 As shared in an email from Paul Geraghty, December 15, 2020.

5 Sometimes I am asked about the religious roots of the architecture
   of selfhood metaphor. Does it work only for Christians? Does it
   draw from Buddhism, Sufism, or other traditions? While I have
   been formed in and by the Christian tradition, and while the

architecture of selfhood metaphor draws from that tradition, dialogue partners from other and no traditions tell me that the architecture of selfhood speaks beyond Christianity. I have, no doubt, been influenced by these dialogue partners as well.

The idea that our selfhood includes the presence of God within us tends to reside in the contemplative tradition within Christianity. Outside of the Christian tradition, Hindus, Buddhists, Muslims, Jews . . . all have some language for the multiple layers of our selfhood. Within the Christian tradition, many Christian contemplatives talk about two selves: the true and false self. Two of the most well-read voices in this regard are Thomas Merton and Richard Rohr, though others such as Beatrice Bruteau, James Finley, and Cynthia Bourgeault also speak to this model. While I affirm the work of these authors and have been influenced by them, I prefer to think of our selfhood as having three layers. If we compare the two models—Merton's/Rohr's with the one presented here—we find that what they call the true self maps most closely onto the deeper self. The idea of the false self maps onto both the descriptive and defended self. Both Merton and Rohr talk about the false self as necessary for development (as children stretch their beings into their descriptive selves) and as eventually false (as allegiance to the descriptive self, in the absence of the deeper self, causes the fall into the defended self). The architecture of selfhood avoids the language of "false self" as it relates to one's descriptors, preserving the absolute acceptability of the descriptive self. This allows the descriptive self to be celebrated for what it is without linking it to falsehood. This allows us to avoid falling into a false binary or dualism where the descriptive self, by association with the defended self, is bad, and the true self is good. Further, by dividing selfhood into three layers, the unity between the descriptive and deeper selves is revealed, reflecting the same unity between humanity and divinity as revealed in Jesus. There is wisdom in practicing fidelity to the deeper self (as Jesus did), and there is wisdom in honoring the unity between the deeper and descriptive selves (as Jesus also did). This, it appears, is the meaning of incarnation: *en*fleshing the breath of God and sharing this breath with the world.

6 For more on this story, see Shmuel Klitzner, *Wrestling Jacob: Deception, Identity, and Freudian Slips in Genesis* (Ben Yehuda Press, 2006).

7 Klitzner, 122–42.

8 Unpublished notes from a Living School Conference, Center for Action and Contemplation, February 2017.

9 Richard Rohr, "Aliveness," Center for Action and Contemplation "Daily Meditations," May 10, 2019, https://cac.org/aliveness-2019-05-10/.

10 Beatrice Bruteau, *Radical Optimism: Practical Spirituality in an Uncertain World* (Boulder, CO: Sentient Publications, 2002), 59. Emphasis in the original.

11 For more, see Beatrice Bruteau, *The Grand Option: Personal Transformation and a New Creation* (Notre Dame, IN: University of Notre Dame Press, 2001), 140–41.

CHAPTER 4

1 Samin Nosrat, *Salt, Fat, Acid, Heat: Mastering the Elements of Good Cooking* (New York: Simon and Schuster, 2017).

2 C. Otto Scharmer, *Theory U: The Social Technology of Presencing* (San Francisco: Berrett-Koehler, 2009), 7.

3 In his book *Forgive for Good: A Proven Prescription for Health and Happiness* (New York: HarperOne, 2003), Fred Luskin notes four barriers to forgiveness: (1) holding people to unenforceable rules; (2) thinking that thinking can change the past; (3) blaming the other for the impact something has had on us; and (4) living from a grievance story. To this list I have added a fifth barrier: (5) seeing the intention of the other as being about us.

4 Interview with "Bishop Michael Curry and Dr. Russell Moore—Spiritual Bridge People," podcast *On Being with Krista Tippett*, December 10, 2020, 50:58, https://onbeing.org/programs/bishop-michael-curry-dr-russell-moore-spiritual-bridge-people/.

5 Joe Schaeffer, Communication and Creative Leadership Workshop, Waterloo, ON, 2002.

CHAPTER 5

1 James Finley, (presentation, Living School Symposium, Center for Action and Contemplation, Albuquerque, NM, August, 2016).

2 Richard Rohr, *Immortal Diamond: The Search for Our True Self* (San Francisco: Jossey-Bass, 2013), xix–xxii.

3 Personal conversation with Paul Hutchinson, August 5, 2020.

4 For more on the difference between shame and guilt, see Brené Brown, *Daring Greatly: How the Courage to Be Vulnerable*

Transforms the Way We Live, Love, Parent, and Lead (New York: Gotham, 2012). See also Brené Brown "Listening to Shame," filmed March 2012 at TED2012, TED video, 20:22, https://www .ted.com/talks/brene_brown_listening_to_shame/.

5 Elizabeth Lesser "The Do No Harm and Take No S*** Practice," interviewed by Tara Brach, November 20, 2020, 18:39, https:// www.youtube.com/watch?v=C6chvht8l4s.

6 James Finley, *Merton's Palace of Nowhere* (Notre Dame, IN: Ave Maria Press, 1978), 30.

7 James Finley, *Following the Mystics through the Narrow Gate* (Albuquerque: Conference at the Center for Action and Contemplation, 2010).

8 As recounted by Cynthia Bourgeault in *The Heart of Centering Prayer: Nondual Christianity in Theory and Practice* (Berkeley: Shambhala, 2016), 14.

9 I developed this version and understanding of the acceptance prayer/mantra to keep what I was learning about meditation alive in the 24/7 of my life. Of course, no idea belongs to any of us individually—I believe I picked up the spirit of this prayer in multiple readings I have done along the way. I have since found resonance for this prayer in the "welcoming prayer" proposed by Thomas Keating and in the impulses of mindfulness.

10 James Finley, *Exploring the Middle Way as a Path to Non-Dual Consciousness,* Living School, Unit 4, Section 1, (Albuquerque: Center for Action and Contemplation, 2017).

11 The mantra is associated with a spiritual discipline known as ho'oponopono. I have borrowed the mantra and applied it to this context.

12 Pema Chödrön, *When Things Fall Apart: Heart Advice for Difficult Times*, 20th anniv. ed. (Berkeley: Shambhala: 2016), 146.

13 Viktor E. Frankl, *Man's Search for Meaning* (Boston: Beacon Press, 1959).

14 Rollo May, *The Courage to Create*, rev. ed. (New York: W. W. Norton; 1994).

15 In this section, I want to acknowledge the influence of Loral Derksen-Hiebert, Jules Hare, and Joan Pries.

16 Jack Kornfield, *After the Ecstasy, the Laundry: How the Heart Grows Wise on the Spiritual Path* (New York: Bantam Books, 2000).

The Author

Betty Pries is cofounder and CEO of Credence & Co., a consulting agency dedicated to working with organizations and their leaders to help them thrive and flourish. With over twenty-eight years of experience coaching, mediating, training, facilitating, and consulting, Betty is highly regarded as a specialist in conflict, change, and leadership. She brings a unique mix of insight, care, facilitation skills, and organizational knowledge to her work with universities, healthcare entities, government agencies, and businesses. In addition, she brings biblical knowledge, theological reflection, and spiritual guidance to her work with congregations and faith-based institutions. The intersection of clients with whom Betty works gives her a unique perspective into a range of concerns that emerge wherever people work and live together. In 2019, she completed a PhD at the Free University Amsterdam (VU) on the topic of conflict transformation and contemplative spirituality.